Country Roads of

OHIO

Country Roads of

OHIO

Drives, Day Trips, and Weekend Excursions

Third Edition

Janet and Gordon Groene

COUNTRY ROADS PRESS
NTC/Contemporary Publishing Group

Library of Congress Cataloging-in-Publication Data

Groene, Gordon.
    Country roads of Ohio : drives, day trips, and weekend excursions /
Gordon and Janet Groene.—3rd ed.
       p.   cm.—(Country Roads)
    Includes index.
    ISBN 1-56626-094-9
    1. Ohio—Guidebooks.   2. Automobile travel—Ohio—Guidebooks.
3. Rural roads—Ohio—Guidebooks. I. Groene, Janet. II. Title.
III. Series : Country Roads (Series).
F489.3.G76   1998
917.7104′43—dc21   99-10339
                                          CIP

Cover and interior design by Nick Panos
Cover illustration copyright © Todd L. W. Doney
Interior site illustrations and map copyright © Leslie Faust
Interior spot illustrations copyright © Barbara Kelley
Picture research by Elizabeth Broadrup Lieberman
Typeset by VARDA Graphics, Inc.

Published by Country Roads Press
A division of NTC/Contemporary Publishing Group, Inc.
4255 West Touhy Avenue, Lincolnwood (Chicago), Illinois 60646-1975 U.S.A.
Copyright © 1999, 1996, 1993 by Janet and Gordon Groene
Printed in the United States of America
International Standard Book Number: 1-56626-094-9

99 00 01 02 03 04 ML 19 18 17 16 15 14 13 12 11 10 9 8 7 6 5 4 3 2 1

To the memory of our Ohio forebears whose names included Groene, Kluth, Klose, Hawkins, Conser, Humphreys, Ruhl, Woolf, and Whiteleather

Ohio Country Roads
(Figures correspond with chapter numbers.)

Contents

Southeast Ohio

Acknowledgments

Special thanks to Scott Dring, public relations manager at the Ohio Division of Travel and Tourism, and to Josh Flory there; Jennifer Wert of the Sandusky/Erie County Visitor and Convention Bureau; the Ottawa County Visitors Bureau; the Peninsula Chamber of Commerce; Amy Warwick of Warwick Public Relations; Christine Zust of Zust & Company; Lois Smith at the Greater Cincinnati Convention and Visitors Bureau; Linda Brejwo of the Marietta/Washington County Convention & Visitors Bureau; Debra Bridge of the Greater Hamilton Convention & Visitors Bureau; Rhonda Cox, executive director of Ohio Valley Visitors Center; Jenny Caze in the Hocking Hills; fellow Ohioan and longtime friend Suzanne Moesly for giving us her cherished copy of *The Ohio Story;* David and Louis Allen of the Mahler Museum in Berea; and to genealogist Robert Irving Hawkins.

Introduction

We grew up in families whose Sunday schedule started with church, followed with dinner and an afternoon ride. Often, dinner and the ride were combined as we sought out yet another country restaurant or picnic site on an unexplored route.

The endless ribbons of Ohio's country roads never failed to beguile us. Familiar roads driven time and again were always new, changing with the seasons. Unfamiliar roads beckoned in abundance. No matter how close we lived to the city, greenbelts were only a short drive away.

Among the miracles of this overpopulated modern world are the metropolitan parks of Ohio. Cleveland is ringed with an emerald necklace: more than 19,000 acres of parks spread their forests and meadows in the shadow of the city. Within them are countless miles of country roads; equestrian paths; paved and wheelchair-accessible hiking and biking trails; plus walking, parcours, jogging, and climbing paths.

The story is repeated in every major Ohio city—Cincinnati, Columbus, Dayton. The cities themselves offer serene parkways and, by venturing only a few miles out of town, you can always pick up a road that leads past cornfields, orchards in bloom, forests alight with autumn color, rocky creeks winking in the sunlight, and villages that seem untouched by the passing years.

Ohio offers such beautiful and varied countryside that a book like this one can hardly begin to tell the story. It is our hope that it will serve as a catalyst and companion for your own explorations of the country roads of Ohio.

It is assumed that, in addition to the general directions given here, you'll have a good Ohio state map as well as county and city maps whenever possible. We also recommend the *Ohio Atlas and Gazetteer* (DeLorme Mapping Company). To simplify road designations, we've used the following abbreviations: I = Interstate; U.S. = U.S. Route or Highway; State = State Route or Highway; County = County Route or Road; Townships = Township Road. Ohio Highway Patrol numbers for communities from Akron to Zanesville are listed individually on the official state map, which is available from 800-BUCKEYE.

General Information

For Ohio information, write the Division of Travel and Tourism, Box 1001, Columbus, OH 43266-0001. Call 800-BUCKEYE.

The Ohio Highway Patrol monitors CB Channel 9 24 hours a day. The toll-free Emergency Highway Hotline is 800-525-5555.

Information about Ohio's more than 300 bed-and-breakfasts is available from Buckeye B&B Reservation Service, Box 130, Powell, OH 43065. Call 740-548-4555 for 24-hour reservation service.

Ohio has 138 miles of rails-to-trails paths along old railroad right-of-ways. Of these, 62 miles are paved. For information, write the Bicycle Transportation Administration, Department of Transportation, 25 South Front Street, Room 418, Columbus, OH 43215. Call 614-466-3741.

For information about privately owned campgrounds offering such amenities as stocked fish ponds, on-site RV rentals, boat rentals, RV repair, baby-sitting, and much more, write the Ohio Campground Owners Association, 3386 Snouffer Road, Columbus, OH 43235. Call 614-764-0279.

Details about winery tours are available from the Ohio Wine Producers Association, 822 North Tote Road, Austinburg, OH 44010. Call 800-227-6972. The state is fourth in the nation in the number of wineries and fifth in wine production.

Ohio Travel Information Centers are always good places to pull over, stretch your legs, and get the latest maps and travel information. Year-round centers are:

On I-90, a mile from the Pennsylvania state line near Conneaut.

On I-70 westbound, in a rest area five miles west of St. Clairsville.

On I-75 northbound and southbound, in the rest area two miles south of the State 63 interchange near Monroe.

In Dayton, at the U.S. Air Force Museum, in the Wright-Patterson Air Force Base off Springfield Street. Take exit 41 off I-70, then State 4 south to Harshaman Road south and turn east on Springfield.

On I-70 eastbound, three miles from the Indiana line near Gettysburg.

At Canton, just off I-77 at the Fulton Road exit next to the Pro-Football Hall of Fame.

On I-80 westbound, a mile from the Pennsylvania line near Hubbard.

On I-77 southbound, in the rest area two miles north of Dover.

On I-71 northbound and southbound, at the rest area five miles north of Lebanon.

On I-77 northbound, at the rest area about six miles north of Marietta.

On I-75 northbound and southbound, at the rest area one mile south of the U.S. 6 interchange near Bowling Green.

State Park Resorts and Lodges

Many state parks offer accommodations at moderate prices. They're enormously popular because they're at the doorstep of the entire park's recreation complex. They're in the middle of nowhere, yet they have many hotel-style amenities such as dining, fitness equipment, lounge/bars, pools, and saunas. Make reservations well in advance. Call 800-282-7275.

State resorts and lodges include Burr Oak in southern Ohio; Deer Creek, south of Mount Sterling; Hueston Woods,

5 miles north of Oxford; Maumee Bay, 10 miles from Toledo; Mohican, southwest of Loudonville; and Punderson Manor, a 31-room, Tudor-style, formerly private home near Newbury.

Outdoor Dramas

Four entertaining outdoor dramas bring history into sharp focus for the country traveler. Sit under the stars on a cool summer night, watching legends come to life before your eyes, and ponder how these same stars saw these same events come true for the first time. They are:

Blue Jacket—The story of a white man who was adopted by the Shawnees and became their war chief. The drama introduces other historical characters, including Simon Kenton and Daniel Boone. Performed at 168 Main Street, Xenia. Call 937-376-4318.

Tecumseh—The life and death of this great Shawnee leader, focusing on his futile attempt to unite all tribes against President Harrison in the struggle for the Northwest Territory. Performed in an amphitheater on Sugarloaf Mountain, Chillicothe. Call 740-775-0700.

Trumpet in the Land—The story of Ohio's first settlement at Schoenbrunn in 1772. It's performed in New Philadelphia. Call 330-339-1132.

The Living Word—A dramatization of the ministry of Jesus Christ. It is presented in Cambridge. Call 740-439-2761.

Fairs, Festivals, and Antique Shows

Ohioans love festivals. Almost every weekend around the calendar, you can find a fair or frolic, pig-roast or taffy-pull somewhere nearby. Many are in villages, hamlets, or mere crossroads, and getting there on country roads is half the fun.

Most events are wheelchair-accessible, and more are being made accessible each year. For dates and a contact name for each event, request the latest quarterly calendar from 800-BUCKEYE.

Ohio's major flea markets are in Aurora, Wilmington, Hartville, South Amherst, and at the fairgrounds in Mansfield, Springfield, Tiffin, Urbana, and Washington Court House.

Central Ohio

The Sweet Corn Festival is held on State 204, Millersport. Eat buttered sweet corn until you are ready to burst, then bust loose on the midway for square dancing, toe tapping to Grand Ole Opry shows, and a parade. Admission. Parking fee.

The Tomato Festival is tomatoes in all forms, from green-tomato pie to tomato butter. There's a grand parade, plus crafts booths and much more. The festival is in Reynoldsburg at the same time the Tomato Show is held in nearby Fredericktown. You can easily do both in the same weekend.

The Popcorn Festival is in Marion, home of the Wyandot Popcorn Museum. Beer gardens, food, free entertainment by big-name stars, parade. Free.

Southeast Ohio

The River Days Festival is held yearly in Portsmouth. Boat races, children's races, parade, arts and crafts. Free.

Ohillco Days in Wellston celebrate Ohio's hill country with a parade and free entertainment. Free.

Marietta's Ohio River Sternwheeler Festival is one of the best events on the river, featuring spectacular sternwheeler races, music, and fireworks. Free.

The American Soya Festival in Amanda is heart-of-America stuff and nonsense at its seed-spitting best. Be there for the parade, square dancing, soybean dishes, and entertainment. Free.

Music in the Park is played Friday at 6:30 P.M. seasonally in downtown Logan at Worthington Park.

The Parade of the Hills is held in August in Nelsonville, where the Paul Bunyan Show is held in October.

The Hocking County Fair is in Logan in September and October, when fall color is at its best. Everyone comes to the Hocking Hills for the Color Caravan.

Winter Cave Hikes are held in Hocking Hills in January, a hushed and uncrowded time to explore the ancient hills.

Northeast Ohio

Oktoberfest at the Lake County Fairgrounds in Painesville is oompah bands, beer, brats, and brouhaha. Admission.

Chickenfest! It's chicken in all its delicious forms, plus entertainment and games—in Barberton. Free.

The Festival of Arts is held on the commons in Toronto. More than 100 craftspeople show their wares while you're serenaded by the sound of music and the smell of down-home foods. Free.

The Baycrafters Renaissance Fayre at Bay Village is a funfest of entertainment, crafts, food, and kidstuff, all tuned to a medieval theme. Admission.

The Great Trail Festival in Malvern serves up kettle-cooked foods, colonial arts and crafts, and living-history demonstrations of life on the Ohio frontier during the French and Indian era. Admission.

The Melon Festival. The town square in Milan spills over with juicy cantaloupes, watermelon, muskmelon, sherbets,

and ice cream for the Melon Festival. It's held in a festival setting with antique cars, races, a grand parade, crafts, and
entertainment. Free.

Antiques in the Woods, on State 7, a mile north of Columbiana, features 90 dealers, all showing their best wares in a
wooded setting. Admission.

The Cochocton County Arts & Crafts Expo is held in a
restored railroad complex on U.S. 36 in West Lafayette. More
than 100 exhibitors are on hand with their handicrafts and
demonstrations. Free.

The Yankee Peddler Festival at Clay's Park in Canal
Fulton is one of the state's biggest and best pioneer festivals.
Admission.

The International Mining and Manufacturing Festival in
Cadiz cuts into a giant coal cake during a long weekend of
folk dancing and costumes from many nations. Free.

Elyria's Apple Festival is everything you expect in an old-
fashioned street fair. Free.

Southwest Ohio

The Ohio Renaissance Festival is a two-month-long extravaganza held five miles east of Waynesville. Jousting and merri-
ment, feasting and crafts. Admission.

The annual Antique & Classic Car Parade in Hamilton
in late July draws about 300 cars to one of America's oldest
antique car events. Free.

South Vienna's Corn Festival honors King Corn with sit-
down dinners, a car show, a parade, flea market, and entertainers. Free.

Trotwood-Madison Heritage Days in Trotwood are a
family weekend with a parade, bike tour, apple cook-off, and
the national kiddie tractor-pull. Free.

More than 1,500 truckers compete in the Mid America Truck Jamboree in the third weekend in June at the Butler County Fairgrounds in Hamilton. See a Show and Shine competition, burnout contests, tough truck competitions, and a manufacturers' midway of displays of trucks and accessories.

Fort Hamilton Days bring arts, feasting, and entertainment to Hamilton the last full weekend in June. Part of the festival is the Main Street Sidewalk and Street Festival, with sidewalk sales, kiddie rides, and demonstrations.

An Antique & Classic Car Parade takes to the streets of Hamilton the fourth Saturday of July. The first Sunday of December, the German Village Historic District of Hamilton has its dazzling Christmas Walk with colors, food, and entertainments under a fairyland of twinkling lights.

Northwest Ohio

The Battle of Lake Erie is relived each year at the Perry's Memorial at Put-in-Bay. Living-history characters camp, fire muskets, and go about their business as though the War of 1812 were still in progress. On Saturday night, there's a concert under the stars. Free.

The Flowing Rivers Festival at Defiance is held on the site of the original Fort Defiance. Free.

Celebrate the annual Autumn Lighthouse Festival at Marblehead Lighthouse with arts, crafts, food, guest artists, and demonstrations at the Keepers House.

Country Roads of

OHIO

1

A Covered Bridge Cavalcade

Getting there: Located on Lake Erie in northeastern Ohio, Ashtabula is on State 11 a few miles north of I-90. It's 65 miles from Cleveland, 205 miles from Columbus, and 312 miles from Cincinnati.

Highlights: Simple country roads studded with covered bridges.

A well-marked route through Ashtabula County makes a circle that you can join anywhere to take a tour of the county's legendary covered bridges. Although the signs stay up throughout the year, the route is especially beautiful in autumn. So we'll begin and end our route in Ashtabula, taking you on the extra, bridgeless leg through the magnificent colors of the Pymatuning Valley, which many people prefer to add when fall color is at its peak.

The tour described covers about 65 to 70 miles and crosses nine bridges. If you want to do it in one day, get an early start to allow time for enjoying the countryside, photographing the covered bridges, and stopping at the many roadside (and bridgeside) stands along the way. A number of the roads are unpaved, and bridges should be crossed at very slow speed, so this isn't a tour to take when you're in a rush.

Considered to be the "covered bridge capital" of the state, Ashtabula has 12 original covered bridges, as well as new ones built in 1983 and 1986 in the old-fashioned style. The bridge at Harpersfield is the longest in the state. Although other areas may have more covered bridges, this county's are actually *working* bridges, and there are more here than anywhere else in the state.

The most festive time to tour the bridges is during the Covered Bridge Festival, the second weekend of October, because the days are packed with activities, including living-history characters and demonstrations, and a parade and festival queen. The number of roadside stands increases, and more places stay open longer hours. It's also a crowded time, which some shunpikers may prefer to avoid.

Winter is the best-kept secret in covered bridge country. Come here in the crackling silence, on a weekday just after a snowfall, when the bridges are mounded with white and the country roads crunch under your tires as you make the first tracks on a frosty morning. As a bonus, you can photograph bridge detail more fully, because the trees that often obscure the views are bare.

Driving south on State 11 and State 46 takes you out of Ashtabula and through Plymouth Township. Continue on State 46 into Jefferson, one of those heart-of-Ohio communities that might be used as a movie set for Midwest, U.S.A.

As you enter town, note the courthouse complex on your right and the date above the door: 1836. Stay on Route 46 until you come to East Cedar Street, then turn left. Here you'll find the quaint and quirky Victorian Perambulator Museum. It is so charming and unusual, it is well worth investigating. Judith Kaminski and Janet Pallo have assembled an impressive collection of babies' and children's clothes and toys, including one of the largest, finest perambulator collections in the nation. Carriages, most of them beautiful examples of wicker

Covered bridge, Ashtabula County

dating from 1860 to 1910, fill the museum. It is open Saturday, 11:00 A.M. to 5:00 P.M., September through May, and other times by appointment.

Also in Jefferson is the Joshua Reed Giddings Law Office Museum, a two-room office built in 1823 and furnished to show what it may have looked like in 1856, when Giddings wrote the draft for the platform of the newly founded Republican Party. The museum is open by appointment.

While in town, railroad buffs can board an old-time train on the AC&J Scenic Line and ride through rolling farmlands and woodlands, where it's not uncommon to see a startled deer or a puzzled rabbit stop feeding to watch you go by.

The engine is a 1951 relic of the old Nickel Plate line, pulling a couple of coach cars and a bright red caboose. To find the station, take East Jefferson Street east off State 46 (Chesnut Street). Cross the tracks and park behind Douglas Lumber. Trains depart at 12:30 P.M., 2:00 P.M., and 3:00 P.M. on Saturday and Sunday, from mid-June through October.

Special Halloween rides are also scheduled. Reservations are not required, but it's wise to call ahead.

Four miles south of Jefferson on State 46 is the Lenox Rural Museum, which has collections of Ohioana and rural memorabilia. It's open on Sunday, 2:00 to 4:00 P.M., from June through September.

From Jefferson head west on State 307 and, in less than a mile, turn right on Doyle Road. Built across Mill Creek by a Vermont carpenter in 1868, this beautiful 94-foot bridge was restored in 1987. If traffic allows it, stop for a look through the windows in the bridge; since the bridge sits at an angle to the road, you'll have a grand vista of the creek.

After crossing the Doyle Road Bridge, turn left on Clay Street, less than a mile away, which parallels I-90. Follow for about five miles before turning left on State 534 to State 307. Grandly spanning the Grand River, the bridge, on Harpersfield Road, was built in 1873. Although surrounding roads were washed out during the violent flood of 1913, this stalwart span survived. West of the bridge is a 17-acre park, ideal for taking photographs, fishing from the dam, or going for a swim.

After the bridge turn left, or east, on State 307, and follow it for three miles to Mechanicsville Road (called Sexton Road to the north), where you'll turn right and cross another bridge almost at once. Bridging the Grand River, this weathered wooden span was built in 1867. The longest single span in the county, it was built in the Howe Truss and Burr Arch manner, which was patented in 1804. The first mill in the county was built here about 1800, on the site of an Indian portage that had been in use for centuries.

Two miles later, turn left on Cold Springs Road for a mile, then right on Tote Street, and left on Schweitzer Road, which takes you to State 45. Turn right, follow for two miles, then go right again, and you'll cross another covered bridge.

Built in 1874, this latticed bridge, also over the Grand River, is supported by a steel underpinning, which was added in 1945. A favorite with bridge buffs, it has constantly been groomed and restored over the years.

Drive past Rice Road and take the next left, which puts you back on Mechanicsville Road, and continue for seven miles. Turn right on New Hudson and cross U.S. 322 onto Wiswell Road. The covered bridge, high over rocky Phelps Creek, is open only to foot traffic. Located in a beautiful park area on the site of ancient Indian fortifications, it is a favorite with photographers.

Built in 1867, it is one of only two bridges in the county that is a designated National Historic Site. Of special interest are the fieldstone abutments, which were cut in the once-busy quarries of Windsor. Also on the corner of Wiswell Road and U.S. 322 is Christ Episcopal Church and Museum, open Sunday afternoons.

Follow the signs to bypass the bridge, and return to State 45 at Orwell on U.S. 322. On State 45 is the Old Brick Museum, open June through September by appointment. Once a private home owned by the same family for five generations, it was built in 1828.

Retrace your route north on State 45 about eight miles through the village of Rock Creek. About four miles later, at the point where you emerged on Schweitzer Road a while back, watch for a right turn on Eagleville Jefferson Road. For a scenic alternative, jog left on Forman at Eagleville and immediately right on Creek Road, which parallels Eagleville Jefferson Road.

You'll go through Jefferson again, this time on East Jefferson Street. Watch for a right turn on South Denmark Road, which twists and meanders to the Mill Creek Bridge, built in 1890. Note the beefy construction. It's typical of covered bridges built in the last half of the 19th century, and is the reason so many bridges in Ashtabula County have survived so well. Continue east one mile after the bridge.

If you can spare the time, go through the beautiful Cherry Valley area, which follows Pymatuning Creek. You'll be rewarded with country scenes that have changed little for a century. The same forests of hickory and beech, maple and oak probably sheltered Indians centuries ago, and today they put on a timeless show for October visitors. You'll drive south on State 193 and, just past State 307, veer left on Hayes Road.

Savor the scenery for the next 8.5 miles until you reach U.S. 322. Turn left and in another mile, go left again on Stanhope-Kelloggsville Road.

Cross State 167 and immediately turn right on Caine Road, and you're back on the covered bridge route to Caine Road Bridge. Built in 1986 using the Pratt Truss method, which is rarely used in wooden bridges, this beautiful example of ancient art and modern craftsmanship takes you across the snaking Ashtabula River.

In two miles you'll come to State 7, turn left, then quickly turn left on Graham Road where you'll pass another covered bridge, which was moved to this park, operated by the Ashtabula Metropolitan Park Commission. It's the perfect setting for a picnic and a grassy stroll. The original bridge was more than a mile downstream from the site, but it was washed away in the flood of 1913.

From Graham Road, turn right to get back on Stanhope-Kelloggsville Road, which takes you 3.5 miles to the next covered bridge at Root Road. This lovely old bridge, built in 1868, was restored in 1983.

Jog right briefly on Root Road and immediately turn left on Reger, which you follow for two miles. Turn right on State 84 for a couple of miles until you reach the crossroads at Bushnell. Turn left on State 7 across Hatch Corners Road, then just past Conneaut Creek turn right on South Ridge, traveling through scenic meadows with serenely grazing milk cows. Proceed east for one mile to a right turn on Middle Road, which takes you across another covered bridge, this one dating to 1868. It's an example of the Howe Truss method, in which iron rods were used with wooden trusses.

Middle Road takes you back to Hatch Corners Road and a right turn. Cross State 7 and in two miles turn right on State Road. Here you'll come to another bridge over Conneaut Creek. Although a bridge has spanned this creek since 1897, this one was built in 1983, using 97,000 board feet of new southern pine and oak.

In less than a mile, turn right on South Ridge Road, then immediately left on Keefus, and left on Creek Road to another covered bridge, soaring above Conneaut Creek. This is a good one to photograph from below as you hike along the colorful creekside trail. Although its exact building date isn't known, it must surely be more than a century old.

An immediate right turn on Amboy takes you back to U.S. 20, then turn left to North Kingsville. Turn left on State 193 and you'll soon see Covered Bridge Pizza on the right side of the road. The owner's hobby is saving real covered bridges and turning them into pizza restaurants. Spicy specialties here are homemade pizzas and breads, chili, pastas, sandwiches, and salads. It's closed Monday.

Continue through Kingsville. Three miles south of town, watch for a right turn on Gageville Plymouth Road at the crossroads of Gageville, then turn right a mile later onto Benetka Road. You'll soon cross the Ashtabula River on another covered bridge.

Built around the turn of the century, this one, with its town lattice design, offers rest rooms, cider and doughnuts, and souvenirs during the festival weekend. The 120-foot span is supported by stalwart stone bases at each end, enabling the bridge to take spring floods in stride.

Turn left on Plymouth Ridge Road and right on Dibble Road, which you come to just after crossing I-90. Then turn left on Dewey, where another covered bridge takes you once again across the winding upper reaches of the Ashtabula River. Named Olin's Bridge, after the family that has owned the adjoining land since 1860, it was built between 1873 and 1875 in town lattice style. If you love river swimming, the water on the west end of this bridge is one of the best spots on the Ashtabula.

A left on Rockwell and a right on Plymouth Ridge brings you back to Ashtabula.

For More Information

Ashtabula County Convention and Visitors Bureau:
  440-275-3202 or 800-337-6746

Covered Bridge Festival, 25 West Jefferson Street, Jefferson 44047 (It's always a good idea to get the latest routing information because bridges are occasionally closed for repair.)

Victorian Perambulator Museum: 440-576-9588

Joshua Reed Giddings Law Office Museum: 440-466-7337

AC&J Scenic Line Railroad: 440-576-6346

Lenox Rural Museum: 440-224-2640

Christ Episcopal Church and Museum: 440-272-5208 or
440-272-5102

Old Brick Museum: 440-437-6519 or 440-437-8333

Covered Bridge Pizza (North Kingsville): 440-224-0497

2

A Lake County Lark

Getting there: Lake County is immediately east of Cleveland, about 250 miles from Cincinnati, and about 100 miles from Columbus. Our tour covers about 40 miles.

Highlights: Lake County's best beaches, greenswards, historic treasures, vineyards, and golf courses, including Quail Hollow.

Lake County sits on the shores of Lake Erie, bordered by Cuyahoga County to the west and Ashtabula County to the east. Its countryside is a favorite getaway for city dwellers who love the bustling beach communities on the lake, quaint but chic bedroom communities, and, upcountry, miles of rolling meadows carpeted in moist, pool table–green grasses. I-90, U.S. 2, and U.S. 20 are its chief east-west arteries and State 44 its north-south aorta.

Enter the county from the east on U.S. 20, west of Geneva. If you're interested in Ohio wineries, turn left on State 528 a few miles past the county line, through the neat, uncrowded farmlands of Madison Township. About two miles south of where you cross I-90, turn left on Griswold, which dead-ends at Emerson; jog left and immediately turn right on Doty. Signs lead you through lush parkways to the Chalet Debonné

Vineyards, where you'll be shown around by a member of the Debevc family.

One of Ohio's finest boutique wineries, Chalet Debonné reflects four generations of wine making. It's now under the direction of Anthony Debevc, who grew up among the vineyards planted by his grandfather. After attending Ohio State, Anthony returned home to plant vinifera and French/American varietals with his father. On the tour, you will see how the wines are made and will be given samples to taste. The wines are available for purchase.

The winery is open from noon to 8:00 P.M., Tuesday through Saturday, with later hours on Wednesday and Friday evening, when there's entertainment. Saturday afternoons are especially festive, with live entertainment and lots of visitors. Although the winery is open all year, winter hours vary, so call ahead.

Retrace your route back to U.S. 20. If you've planned in advance to attend a production at Rabbit Run, a summer theater housed in a barn in a woodsy, farmland setting, turn right on Haines Street (about four miles west of the county line) and left on Chapel Road to the theater. To see what's playing (and cooking) call 440-428-7092.

If you've always wondered about nuclear power, the Perry Nuclear Power Plant invites visitors to "see what clean, safe nuclear power is all about." The plant is located in Perry, approximately 40 miles east of Cleveland. From State 2, drive 35 miles until Route 2 turns into U.S. 20. Stay on U.S. 20 to Center Road and turn left. The two-hour walking tour is offered Monday through Thursday 8:00 A.M. to 2:00 P.M. and must be scheduled at least two weeks ahead.

As you enter Painesville Township on U.S. 20, just past the Perry Mobile Home Park on your left, watch for the fork

where State 2 separates from U.S. 20. Take State 2 and the first exit, then turn right on County 538. This goes to one of Lake Erie's oldest and most picturesque harbors.

Turn right on East Street and left on Second Street, which brings you to the old lighthouse—now the Fairport Marine Museum. This National Historic Landmark was the first lighthouse marine museum in the nation. The lighthouse keeper's house and pilothouse of the old *S.S. Frontenac* are also part of the complex.

Its collections include navigation instruments, charts, old maps showing the course of the Grand River (which has changed over the years), shipboard memorabilia, plus samples of the iron ores that were once loaded here by the thousands of tons. Also on display are Indian relics from before the days when Fairport Harbor was one of Lake Erie's first and most important harbors.

The museum is open from Memorial Day through Labor Day on Wednesday, Saturday, Sunday, and legal holidays from 1:00 to 6:00 P.M. A small admission is charged.

Fairport Harbor has a large fleet of charter boats with knowledgeable crews if you want to book an offshore fishing adventure.

Return to State 2, pass the State 44 south exit (unless you want to spend a few days golfing at Quail Hollow, which is south on State 44 to the I-90 interchange), and exit on State 44 North, following it for two miles to Headlands Beach State Park, where there is plenty of parking.

This is really two parks: the popular beach state park with its manicured sands, picnic areas, concession stands, and lively fishing from the breakwall; and, to the east, Headlands Dunes State Nature Preserve. By walking the pass less traveled, you'll see the wild side of the lakefront, where untamed dunes have been allowed to sprout beach grasses. These in turn catch blowing sand, creating valleys and hollows in an ever-changing triumph of nature's sculpting talents.

To find the area, walk to the east end of the beach as directed by signs that point to Fishing Access. Follow the trail through the willows and scrubby wild cherry trees and you're on the leeward side of the breakwater, gazing across at the lighthouse at Fairport Harbor.

If you're a bird-watcher, seek out this area at sunrise and sunset, especially in spring and fall when wave after wave of different birds come through in pairs, then wedges, then huge squadrons. A large area of wetlands immediately southwest of the state park is a wildlife reserve sheltering hundreds of species of birds, insects, and small animals.

Headlands State Park is the beginning (or end) of the Buckeye Trail, a 500-mile path that ends at the Ohio River in Cincinnati. It's well marked by blue blazes on trees and other waypoints, so strike off if the mood is upon you and get back to us when you return.

Leaving the Headlands by heading south on State 44, keep a lookout to your right for wildlife sightings in the marshes. Turn right on State 283 past Mentor Harbor and its yacht club and you'll run into a tiny postage stamp–size park directly on the lake. It's on your right.

Drop south from the park on Andrews Road one mile to Lakeshore Boulevard, turn right and go about a mile, then turn left on State 306. It's about three miles to U.S. 20, where you'll take a left. Now watch for Lawnfield, two miles farther on your left—a 30-room, white-frame Victorian mansion. It was the home of President James A. Garfield, who moved there in 1876 with his wife, mother, and five children.

One of the most poignant items on display here is a waxed funeral wreath that was sent by Queen Victoria when word of Garfield's assassination reached England. An Ohio native and Civil War hero, Garfield campaigned from here, speaking from his front porch during the election of 1880. He won in a bitter contest but his term was brief. On July 2, 1881, he was shot at a railroad station in Washington, D.C., by a disappointed office seeker, Charles Guiteau. Garfield lingered for two months, and died in September.

It was four years before Mrs. Garfield could bring herself to alter his beloved Lawnfield. Finally, a wing was added to house his Memorial Library, additional bedrooms, and a room that now serves as a gift shop. The museum is open Tuesday through Saturday 10:00 A.M. to 5:00 P.M., and Sunday noon to 5:00 P.M. Admission is charged.

Leaving Lawnfield and heading east on U.S. 20, turn left on Center Street (State 615) if you are an art buff. Gallery One, which is open every day, claims to be America's largest. Located at 7003 Center Street, the gallery exhibits the works of dozens of artists. Often a famous artist is on hand for a one-man or one-woman show and will gladly chat with visitors.

Return south on Center Street; after passing I-90, the road very soon dead-ends into Chillicothe Road. Turn left, then immediately turn right onto Baldwin Road, which takes you through the hilly Chagrin River valley. It's only two miles to the Holden Arboretum—one of the Midwest's most dazzling and varied preserves. An entire wild kingdom covering more than 3,000 acres, it is planted with dogwood, azaleas, and trees of all colors, shapes, and sizes. There are ponds and gardens, picnic grounds, and walking trails with something in bloom from first blush of spring until late frost. Start at the reception center, where you can pick up maps and learn more about the collections here.

The show begins in March with the sweet drip of the sugar maple. By April and May, wildflowers are erupting along the 20 miles of trails, and crab apples are abloom in the woodlands. The lilac show in May is worth a special trip, but don't fail to come back a few weeks later when rhododendrons and azaleas steal the spotlight. By August, pastels give way to bolder colors—brilliant red mums and garish marigolds, which gently fade to bronze as the weather chills and the trees turn scarlet and gold.

The Holden Arboretum is open daily except Mondays, Christmas, and New Year's, from 10:00 A.M. to 5:00 P.M. Admission is modest; children under age six are admitted free, and senior citizens get a discount.

From the arboretum, turn left on Sperry Road and follow it to Booth Road. Turn right on Booth, right on Baldwin, right on Little Mountain Road, and right again on King Memorial Road. The Lake County History Center will be on your right.

Start at the museum in the Shadybrook House for a 15-minute audiovisual presentation on the history of the county. If you like, you can rent an audiocassette player and a tape to listen to as you walk through the rest of the complex.

While you're there, tour the Cobb-Burridge House, built about 1840, a fine example of the Greek Revival style. An easy walk around the grounds takes you past two Native American constructions, a log house typical of the turn of the 19th century in Ohio, an 1830 one-room schoolhouse, and a barn. Classes and workshops are often going on, so feel free to peek in to see people who are learning to use traditional tools to make traditional crafts.

After leaving Mooreland Mansion, retrace your route to State 84, turn left, and proceed to State 306. Take a left, noting the turn-of-the-century Colonial Revival house, now a part of Lakeland Community College. Furnished in fine Second–Empire pieces from the early 20th century, it's open by appointment. Modest admission is charged. Call ahead.

Now continue south to the Mormon Temple. Modern Mormons know Kirkland, Ohio, as the home of the first church built by followers of Mormon founder Joseph Smith, Jr. A National Historic Landmark built between 1833 and 1836, the temple on State 306 is still maintained by the reorganized branch of the Mormons. It is open Monday through Saturday from 9:00 A.M. to 5:00 P.M., and Sunday 1:00 to 5:00 P.M. It's closed Thanksgiving, Christmas, and New Year's.

Here at State 306 and Chillicothe Road is another Mormon landmark, the Newel K. Whitney Store and Museum. In a one-hour tour, you'll be told the story of Joseph Smith and the founding of his church. Once Smith's home, this museum has been restored as an 1830 store and post office.

Only six miles south on State 306 is one of those family attractions that's too good to miss. In fact, you may want to devote an entire day to Lake Farmpark. To get there, drive south on State 306 to U.S. 6 (Chardon Road), then turn left and it will be on your right.

This is the kind of place parents and grandparents like to take children to show them what country life was like in the good ol' days. Serious gardeners and farmers will also enjoy the 235 acres of meadows and woodlands, farm fields and pastures. Displays include antique and modern farm equipment, more than 50 breeds of livestock, simple gardens, and lavish crops. Take time to see it all at a leisurely pace. Smell the flowers, milk a cow, and pet a lamb.

There's also a theater, gift shop, and restaurant at Lake Farmpark, which is open 9:00 A.M. to 5:00 P.M. daily. (Closed Christmas and New Year's Day and on Monday during January through March.) Admission is charged, but children under five enter free, and discounts apply for senior citizens and youths aged 6 through 18.

Continuing back north on State 306, cross I-90 and a few hundred feet later turn left on State 84 (Johnnycake Ridge Road). In two miles, you'll turn right onto Shankland Road, where the Little Red Schoolhouse is found at 5040. Moved here in 1975, this authentic school dates back to 1901.

Stop to see the gift shop, a kitchen furnished faithfully to the period, a parlor and workshop typical of the early 20th century, and a historical library. For information about tours and hours, call ahead.

A few blocks north on Shankland brings you to U.S. 20 (Mentor Avenue) and the drive back east across the county. We've saved these sites for the way home. Just before reaching State 44, note the county fairgrounds, which will be of interest only if something is going on at the time. The county fair, an old-fashioned extravaganza featuring everything from a midway to pies and pigs to quilts, is held at the end of August, and an Oktoberfest is held on Labor Day weekend. For schedules of other events, contact the Lake County Visitors Bureau.

A few blocks past State 44 on your left, watch for Rider's Inn at 792 Mentor Avenue. This regal old inn has been hosting wayfarers since 1812, when it was opened by Joseph Rider. The inn sheltered runaway slaves before the Civil War, and was later used as a retreat for weary Civil War soldiers home from battle.

Dinners in Mistress Suzanne's dining room feature game, fish, meats, and fowl, all prepared to original, 19th-century recipes. Desserts are presented tableside. Mr. Joseph's English Pub is a friendly place to take an aperitif in front of the stone fireplace, or an unhurried after-dinner drink with darts or puzzles. Sunday brunch is a time-honored tradition.

Take bed and breakfast (in bed) in rooms furnished with antiques. Rooms have private baths, telephones, and room service. If you want to watch television, join other guests in the cozy gathering room. It's one of the few inns where pets are sometimes allowed. Your hosts, Elaine Crane and her mother, Elizabeth Roemish, have a dog and a cat, so discuss with them your needs if you travel with a pet.

Your hosts can also steer you to the best sailing in summer and good cross-country ski trails in winter.

Farther east on U.S. 20 is a very good Indian Museum in Kilcawley Center at Lake Erie College. It's open September through June, with exhibits relating to area archaeological sites, as well as other Indian discoveries throughout Ohio and North America.

A few blocks more brings you to the Lake County Courthouse on your right. A stunning classical French design, it was built in 1907. If you continue traveling east on U.S. 20, you'll come back to your starting point. If you'd prefer to take I-90 east, turn right on State Street just after the courthouse. A few blocks later, veer right on Bank Street then left for a few hundred feet, where you'll join State 84. In about two miles, signs will lead you to an I-90 interchange and Masons Landing, a scenic park on the Grand River. Stop here for a picnic or take a brisk hike before hitting the interstate.

For More Information

Lake County Visitors Bureau (Painesville): 440-354-2424 or 800-368-LAKE

Chalet Debonné Winery: 440-466-3485

Rabbit Run Theater: 440-428-7092

Perry Nuclear Power Plant: 440-280-5352

Fairport Marine Museum: 440-354-4825

Lawnfield: 440-255-8722

Gallery One: 440-255-1200 or 800-621-1141

Holden Arboretum: 440-946-4400

Lakeland Community College: 440-953-7000

Mormon Temple: 440-256-3318

Newel K. Whitney Store and Museum: 440-256-9805

Lake Farmpark: 440-256-2122 or 800-366-FARM

Little Red Schoolhouse: 440-875-3740

Rider's Inn: 440-354-8200

Lake Erie College Indian Museum: 440-352-1911

Glidden House (Cleveland): 440-231-8900

Stouffer Tower City Plaza (Cleveland): 440-696-5600

3

The Comely Cuyahoga Valley

Getting there: From Cleveland, take I-77 south to Rockside Road, then go east to Canal Road, which takes you south to the Canal Visitors Center. From Akron, go north on Akron-Cleveland Road (State 8), then left on State 303 to the Happy Days Visitors Center. Pick up literature and maps, and look at exhibits relating to the park's history.

Highlights: A 33,000-acre green corridor between Cleveland and Akron made up of miles of hiking and biking trails, a major ski area, and a wealth of historic sites, plus 90 miles of the bending Cuyahoga River. Blossom Music Center, Hale Farm and Village.

Winter is the Cuyahoga Valley's time to sleep, which also makes it a silent, secret time for walking or skiing snowy trails. Look for footprints of raccoon and deer in the snow and bright red cardinals perched on snow-crusted branches. Fun-seekers congregate at the Brandywine or Boston Hills ski centers and on any open hills where a sled or toboggan can catch a ride. When spring comes on with a rush of melting snow and quickened waters, all nature seems suddenly to demand attention. Maple trees put out a fringe of red; violets bloom; willows sprout leaves of palest green;

spring-beauties peek out of beds formed by last year's fallen leaves.

Summer is everyone's favorite time, but the valley is so vast that visitors on the most crowded days can still find quiet glens in the shade of ancient sycamores or fragrant meadows dappled with sunshine. In autumn, uplands turn lavender as asters bloom, and lowlands turn rusty with ripening cattails. Trees burn red and yellow while Queen Anne's lace forms borders around fields of blue chicory.

For the motorist, the beauty and the irony of the Cuyahoga Valley National Recreational Area is that it is bisected by the Cuyahoga River. If you stay only on the river-hugging roads, you'll miss much of what this urban park has to offer. Some backtracking and dead-heading are not just inevitable, they are part of the fun.

It all comes back to the river, which was scraped out of the earth millennia ago by glaciers. Bison and puma, wolf and bear prowled its forested banks. Prehistoric Indians considered it neutral territory, free for all peoples to make their way from Lake Erie down the Cuyahoga to the Tuscarawas River and south via the Ohio River.

The first settlers built cabins in 1786 where Tinkers Creek meets the Cuyahoga. (The site is near the Canal Visitors Center, which will be one of the important waypoints when you come here.) Ten years later, when Moses Cleaveland laid out the Western Reserve, he knew that the Cuyahoga would remain a major artery. By 1827 a canal had been completed between Cleveland and Akron, using the Cuyahoga's waters. The canal's fate was sealed in 1880 when the rail line opened, and now it, too, is a half-forgotten steel trail used only by excursion trains hauling sightseers.

Save an hour or more for the visitors center, which adjoins the Twelve-Mile Lock, so called because it is 12 miles from Lake Erie. Open daily, the center has exhibits, special programs on natural history, rangers to answer your questions, and an audiovisual program explaining the role of the canals. Once called Hell's Half Acre, the locktender's domain has served as a dance hall, general store, saloon, and private home.

Leave the center on Tinkers Creek Road, looking back to your right for a view of an enormous aqueduct. An engineering marvel during the canal days, it carried water, complete with boats, across Tinkers Creek. Continue to the Gorge Parkway, where you'll soon see picnic tables right and left, then an overlook to the left.

Within the next few miles, watch for two other picnic areas on the left side of the parkway. Hungry or not, take every available chance to pull over, savor the nature show, and gaze down on Tinkers Creek Gorge, which has been designated a National Natural Landmark. Off to the right, watch for breathtaking Bridal Veil Falls.

Take Egbert Road back west to Alexander Road and turn left on Canal Road. Here you'll find the last operating mill on the river, built in 1853 as Wilson's Mill and later named for the Alexanders. Water-powered mills were, of course, common along the river in the days before electricity. This one was run by a turbine rather than the familiar waterwheel. Adjoining the mill, see the remains of Twelve-Mile Lock. Nearby is the Frazee House, open to the public. Built in the 1820s and restored in 1992-93, it was one of the first homes in the area. Having witnessed the valley go from the stagecoach era to the canal days, the Frazee House has been turned into an Ohio and Erie Canal museum.

The mill looks out over an area called The Meadow, a former dump site that has been returned to its native switchgrass. Today it supports a population of fox, raccoon, grouse, and deer.

Walk south along the canal for a couple of miles, savoring the memories of the old towpath and the beauty of the Pinery Narrows. The slopes here, bracketing the river in a narrow, 1,000-foot channel, were once forested solidly with giant white pines, which were logged long ago for ship masts. Watch for blue heron, which breed in this area in nests that look like large piles of sticks.

The towpath is actually a foot trail along the length of the canal, except for an impassable area where the interstates cross the park between the towns of Boston and Peninsula. Walk it for as far as you have the time.

If you're looking for a serious hike or bike ride, the longest trail begins on Brandywine Road near Happy Days Visitors Center and winds north through the Gorge, ending in Bedford. Or, take any of the shorter trails found throughout the park. To explore the park on horseback, outfit at the Brecksville Stables or Wetmore Bridle Trails. The park also hosts parts of the Buckeye Trail, which crosses the entire state of Ohio. Maps of this trail are sold in visitors centers.

Continuing south on Chaffee Road, turn right on State 82 to cross the river and enter the Brecksville Reservation. The bridge itself is a landmark. Soaring and graceful, it was built in 1931 of concrete, which at that time was a new material, providing the strength needed for a bridge but without the thick, ponderous structure that had been required to achieve the same strength in brick or stone.

Follow signs to the Brecksville Nature Center, where naturalists give talks and show exhibits on the area. Sleepy Hollow, a golf course, is a popular cross-country ski area in winter.

Two points of interest in the Brecksville Reservation are Deer Lick Cave and, south on Riverview Road, the ghost town of Jaite. Built in 1906 to house mill workers, it was typical of company towns of those days, complete with a company store. The buildings have been adapted for use as head-quarters by the National Park Service.

Continuing south on Riverview, you'll see the Boston Mills Ski Resort on your right. Turn right on Boston Mills Road and follow for a mile to Blue Hen Falls. Then backtrack on Boston Mills Road to cross the river again. As you enter Boston, try to picture it as the boomtown it was when Jim Brown, a notorious counterfeiter who died in 1865, made millions of dollars here.

Once a thriving community of boatyards, shops, a tavern, and a hotel, Boston was swept almost completely away by the flood of 1913. Today it's again a quiet settlement, offering views of the remains of the canal and the old company store.

If you jog north on Stanford Road, you'll see the stately old Stanford House, which belonged to one of the Cuyahoga's original settlers. It's now a youth hostel. Following Stanford Road as it takes a sharp right turn, you'll come to Brandy-wine Falls cascading down the rim of the valley. Long before the canal era, a village stood here, its mills turned by the power of the falls.

Return now to the west bank of the river and head south on Riverview to Peninsula, named because it really *was* a penin-sula, formed as the snaking Cuyahoga curled back upon itself. In the early canal days, the settlement was as busy and important as Cleveland, but the thriving boomtown faded when the railroad stole its thunder in 1880.

Today the entire community is a National Historic District. Peninsula is a favorite haunt of architecture buffs, canal and rail fanciers, and antique hunters. Its charmingly restored streets set the scene for shops, restaurants, and nostalgia.

A favorite stop is Fisher's Cafe and Pub at 1607 Main Street. Unassuming and homey, it's open every day from 7:00 A.M. through dinner.

Just south of Peninsula is Deep Lock, which had a lift of 17 feet. The sandstone quarry nearby, now Quarry Park, belonged to Ferdinand Schumacher of the Quaker Oats fortune, who mined quarry stone here to use in his gristmills in Akron. In springtime, the area is alight with migrating warblers.

Quarry Park has picnic areas and hiking trails. To go fishing, head one mile west on Major Road, and turn south to Oak Hill.

If you're here in March or April, go west from Peninsula on State 303 and walk the Daffodil Trail, which is bounded by Brush Road, Black Road, State 303, and I-77. The dazzling appearance of thousands of daffodils lasts for about six weeks. The area, known as Furnace Run Park, also offers picnicking and pond fishing in summer; skiing and ice-skating in winter.

The quickest way to get to the next point of interest is to hop on I-77, head south to the Wheatley Road exit, turn south on Revere Road, and follow it to Ira Road, which leads east into Hale Farm and Village.

At the visitors center here, you'll be greeted by a roaring fire in the huge, two-sided fireplace, and appetizing smells wafting from the kitchen, where burgers, onion rings, pie, and other simple foods are offered for sale.

Watch the orientation movie before exploring the village at your own pace. It can take an entire day, so don't rush it. The farm buildings are original but most of the "village" buildings were brought in from other places in Ohio to find new life here in a living museum. The farm dates to 1810, the original farmhouse to 1826, and it is all operated today by the Western Reserve Historical Society much as it would have been 150 years ago.

Throughout the village, people are going about their business as they would have in the mid-1800s. Land deals are
made, church attended and (real) weddings held, crops
planted and harvested, cider squeezed, and candles dipped.

Hale Farm is officially open May 20 through November 1,
but many special events are held throughout the year, including a Dickens Christmas and maple sugaring in February and
March. You may want to call ahead to see what's going
on when, and make a special trip to the place. Admission is
charged.

The last covered bridge in this area spans Furnace Run,
north of Hale Farm and Village. Nearby and undergoing
restoration is the village of Everett. It also became known as
Johnnycake Lock because it was here that railroad passengers
and crew lived on johnnycakes, the only food they had left
during the lean days after the 1828 flood.

Just east of Hale Farm and Village, another old quarry
has been turned into a fishing lake and picnic area. The
marshland along the river is alive with beavers, which can be
seen working from dawn to dark building dams, gnawing
down trees, thwacking the water with their tails, and leading
busy-beaver lives.

Cross the river on Yellow Creek/Bath Road, then turn left
(north) on Akron-Peninsula Road, where you'll find Hampton
Hills Park. This is a fine place to picnic, play ball, and hike
along Adam's Run through bowers of black walnut and
sycamore trees. Wildflowers bloom from the earliest spring
bluebells through the last goldenrods of autumn.

Off Steel Corners Road are Blossom Music Center, famed
for its summer outdoor concerts by the Cleveland Orchestra,
and Porterhouse Theater, owned by Kent State University,
where summer presentations range from Shakespeare to
Broadway.

Proceeding north on Akron-Cleveland Road, you'll come
to Happy Days Visitors Center, a good starting point for

touring what is called the Virginia Kendall Area of the park. The building, built in the 1930s by the Civilian Conservation Corps, was a camp for inner-city children long before the Happy Days of Fonzie fame. Maps and other Cuyahoga Valley literature are available here, where you also can see films, slide shows, and exhibits interpreting the park.

Hampton Hills Park is a complete recreation area, where you can hike trails among rock ledges that lead to Ice Box Cave. In winter, the fields and trails are perfect for cross-country skiing and snowshoeing. In summer, it's a favorite spot for group picnics and family reunions in one of the picnic shelters.

From Happy Days, it's a short drive north on State 8 to rejoin the Ohio Turnpike, or go west on State 303 to I-275, and you're on your way.

Or, head south on State 8 to Talmadge Avenue, turning right, then right again on Portage Path—one of Akron's most elegant old streets. Lined with big trees and lovely old homes, it includes one of the Midwest's great estates, Stan Hywet Hall at 714 North Portage Path.

This is a destination for visitors from around the world, so allow plenty of time for it during your visit to the Cuyahoga Valley. Home tours are given Tuesday through Saturday from 10:00 A.M. to 4:00 P.M. and Sunday from 1:00 to 4:00 P.M. In summer, the grounds stay open until 9:00 P.M. Admission is charged.

Built as a family home by Frank A. Seiberling, cofounder of Goodyear Tire and Rubber Company, the sprawling brick mansion rivals many of England's stately manors for space, elegance, and fidelity to its Tudor theme. One room was, in fact, brought complete from a house in England that was about to be torn down.

The place isn't to everyone's taste—it is dark and imposing—but we liked the way it combined the Tudor style with furnishings and memorabilia that show how the family actually lived here from 1915 until Seiberling died in 1955. Family photos and accessories from the 20s and 30s give some of the rooms a lived-in look.

The gardens are the estate's real glory, however. Originally 3,000 acres, the grounds now cover 70 lovingly landscaped acres. Every tree, path, fence, and stone was placed with artistry and care. Each planting was planned and nurtured. You can come here every day spring through fall and see a different garden as blooms come and go.

If you didn't bring a camera, buy one of the disposable models, because the scene is irresistible. Allées lead from the house, creating portraits of sun and shadow. The rhododendron allée explodes with color in early summer; the birch allée looks out for miles across the valley.

There is a walled English garden, acres of green lawn, miles of bright borders, a serene Japanese garden, a dell with an amphitheater where one of the Seiberling daughters was married in 1919, a lagoon, a rose garden, another garden for ornamental shrubs, and a cutting garden for the arrangements that are placed throughout the house. Year-round, flowers grow inside the conservatory, where waterfalls and fountains flow.

Study the map you're given when you arrive to plan your tour. If you can't do it all, take the Highlights Garden Tour, for those who want to hit the most important spots, or the Limited Walking Tour, for those who can't walk the long distances required to see all the gardens.

For More Information

Greater Cleveland Convention and Visitors Bureau:
   216-621-4110 or 800-468-4070

Cuyahoga Valley National Recreation Area: 440-526-5256 or
800-445-9667

Akron Area Convention and Visitors Bureau: 330-376-5550

Cuyahoga Valley Line Railroad: 330-657-2000 or 800-468-4070

Fisher's Cafe and Pub (Peninsula): 330-657-2651

Hale Farm and Village: 330-666-3711

Blossom Music Center: 216-566-8184 (Cleveland) or
330-920-8040 (Akron)

Stan Hywet Hall: 330-638-5533

4

Ambling Through Amish Country

Getting there: Millersburg is about 70 miles south of Cleveland and 75 miles northeast of Columbus.

Highlights: Amish crafts and country folks, traditional farms and wagons out of another century in a hilly, Swiss-like setting.

Most of the routes included here take you through working farmlands where plowing and planting, harvesting, and hay-making go on with Swiss clocklike precision, using horse-drawn farm machines.

Acres of green peppers, seas of squash, and miles of green beans are planted here to supply supermarkets throughout the state. Winter brings sleds and skis to the slopes, which reminded early settlers of the Alps they had left behind in the old country. The Clear Fork Ski Area is between Loudonville and Lexington, just off I-71.

Charmed by the quiet, old-fashioned dignity of Amish ways, Ohio travelers love to drone quietly down the country roads of counties with large Amish populations. There's no need to hurry. When you're stuck on a narrow road behind a horse and wagon (or a tour bus), the world's worries are replaced by the calm of another, slower-paced age.

On the north side of Millersburg on State 83, you'll pass the Victorian House, which has 28 rooms filled with gorgeous antiques contributed by local citizens. Built in 1900 for a wealthy industrialist and his family of 12 children, it is a masterful example of Queen Anne design, scrupulously restored and maintained.

Victorian House is open limited hours, Tuesday through Sunday. Call ahead, 330-674-3975. Admission is charged.

Rastetter Woolen Mill in Millersburg is the county's oldest business. Until it was sold in the 1990s, it was operated by five generations of the same family. Stop Tuesday through Saturday to see the braided rugs, hand-woven rag rugs, woolen comforters, hand-stuffed goose-down pillows, and a wealth of woolens.

From Millersburg, drive northeast on Route 241, then right on County 203. Honey Run Quilts and Crafts is one of the dozens of roadside shops where you can see the unique, caring craftsmanship for which the Amish are known. Dozens of such shops dot this area, too many to list. Stopping for them is part of the fun of traveling the slow lane through Holmes County.

When you reach County 201, turn right, then left on State 39 and State 62 into Berlin. Dutch Country Kitchen has a salad bar, and hearty Amish foods that you can order by the serving or by the bowlful, family style.

Stop by the Mennonite Information Center on County 77 between U.S. 62 and State 39 to get a big welcome, use the clean and appealing rest rooms, and select maps and brochures. A 265-foot historical cyclorama explains the Amish, Hutterite, and Mennonite faiths.

If you like buying foodstuffs in bulk, this is the place to pig out, stock up, and save big on spices, cheeses, and other nonperishable staples as well as fresh meats. Berlin Bulk

Foods is next to Nature's Paradise just behind the little village park on the square. It's an interesting place to stop for provisions by the pound, barrel, and gross.

The entire main route through Berlin is, in fact, lined with shops of all kinds. Any time is a good time to stroll from shop to shop, but the Christmas season is especially festive and frosty, a time to enjoy hot cider, carriage rides, caroling, and lights.

A mile east of Berlin on State 39, the Amish Farm opens its doors to give you a taste of Amish life. First there's a 20-minute presentation explaining Amish customs, then a buggy ride, hayride, tour, and other down-home fun.

U.S. 62 breaks off to the left, taking you to Bunker Hill and then into Winesburg. Across from the water tower, the Winesburg Craft House sells handmade dolls and furniture, baskets, rocking horses, dollhouse furniture, and hickory rockers. It's closed Sunday. Among other shops in the hamlet is Winesburg Collectibles, housed in a store that was built in 1895. Clocks, crocks, and creations of all sorts with an Amish accent are here for your choice.

If you want to extend your trip, continue northeast on U.S. 62 into Wilmot and turn left on U.S. 250, which takes you to The Wilderness Center and its 10 miles of nature trails.

South of Wilmot on U.S. 62 you'll pass Alpine-Alpa, an entertainment-dining center with two animated Alpine dioramas and the world's largest cuckoo clock, plus cheese in the making, and a gift shop. Also on U.S. 62 in Wilmot is the Amish Door, serving traditional Amish cooking in a barn. It's open daily 7:00 A.M. to 8:00 P.M. (winter) and to 9:00 P.M. (summer).

Retrace your route on U.S. 62, then turn south on State 515 through the town of Trail toward Walnut Creek. Between these two settlements, stop for a tour of Yoder's Amish Home.

You'll be shown through an 1866 Amish-Mennonite home and a modern, 10-room Old Order Mennonite home. Ramble the 116-acre working farm, help stir the apple butter, pet the animals, or take a ride in a horse-drawn buggy or hay wagon. It's open daily except Sunday, mid-April through October.

About the Amish

A culture, a religion, and a way of life—the Amish folkways you'll observe in this region began in Europe in the 16th century, when religious groups splintered after the Reformation over such issues as whether baptism should be done on infants or adults, and whether Christians should serve in the military. Persecuted for their beliefs, Amish families began to emigrate to America.

Groups represented in this area today include the Old Order Amish, New Order Amish, Beach Amish, Amish Mennonites, and conservative Mennonites. Subtle differences in dress tell the Amish immediately about each other; the outsider may find it more difficult to note the placement of a pin here, an apron there, and the significance of a black shawl or a white cape. Even the men's suspenders, which may make an H, an X, or a Y in back, differentiate the sects.

Most of the children now attend public schools, but you'll also see a few of the one-room parochial schools preferred by more conservative families. Even today, many local children consider their education fulfilled when they finish the eighth grade or reach the age of 14, whichever comes first.

Zippers, like other newfangled devices, are not accepted by the Amish. Their simple clothes are fastened by hooks, snaps, buttons, or Velcro. Men wear big-brimmed hats; women, head-hugging white bonnets. On Sunday they stroll to church in somber black.

You'll find many of the businesses closed on Sunday; some do not have telephones. Cows are milked by hand, homes are lit by lanterns, and pickup trucks are eschewed in favor of horse-drawn wagons. It's a way of life that outsiders often envy and should always respect as an alternative lifestyle, not a tourist attraction. Be sure to ask permission before taking a picture; some Amish prefer not to be photographed.

Next to the post office in Walnut Creek, the German Culture Museum is devoted to the Swiss and German heritage of the local people. It's open from mid-June through October; closed Monday.

Just off State 39 on State 515, Der Dutchman is one of the area's biggest and boldest restaurants and gift complexes, its deck overlooking the valley that locals call Genza Bottom. After dining, "set a spell" on one of the hickory rockers on the long front porch. The restaurant is closed Sunday. Across the street is the Carlisle House, a Victorian showplace now turned into a shop selling furniture, crafts, dolls, and collectibles.

A half mile west of Walnut Creek on State 39, there's an enormous indoor flea market featuring, of course, Amish quilts and furniture. It's open April through November; closed December through March. Call the Holmes County Chamber of Commerce, 216-674-3975, for hours.

State 39 takes you east to Sugarcreek. The Alpine Hills Historical Museum here is open April through November; there is no admission fee. Old-fashioned country cooking is the fare at the Swiss Hat, and the all-you-can-eat buffets on Sunday are worth the entire trip.

Backtrack on State 39 and turn left on County 114 into Farmerstown, then turn right on State 557 into Charm. The name says it all. Miller's Dry Goods has 2,000 bolts of calicos and plains to choose from. Chances are, most of the customers will be Amish ladies choosing plains for their quilts and the family clothes they make by hand and on treadle sewing machines. You're welcome to ask for advice about making your own quilts, too. Miller's is open 8:00 A.M. to 5:00 P.M. daily, except Sunday.

Two and a half miles south of Charm on State 557 is the Countryview Inn, a peaceful bed-and-breakfast. Here you'll sleep under a handmade Amish quilt and wake up to a hearty, farmhand-size Amish breakfast. State 557 takes you north and past the Chalet in the Valley. Swiss, Austrian, and American-Amish foods are served while you gaze out over the Doughty Valley.

Turn left on U.S. 62 and follow it south out of Millersburg for eight miles into Killbuck. As the name implies, this is prime hunting country where, since pioneer times, deer harvests have been plentiful. The Killbuck Valley Museum here has displays that go back to the dawn of valley history. Start at the Ice Age and work forward through the Indians, old tools, the railroads, and 19th-century tools. The museum is open May through October; there is a modest admission fee. Call for hours.

If you like herbs, birdhouses, wildflower wreaths, and other country items, head south on State 60 to Bittersweet Farm, open daily March through December; closed January and February.

Turn north now on State 60 and follow it back to State 39, heading west through farm country with neat white homes and flower-filled dooryards, silos fat with corn, and rolling fields of black soil plowed in perfect rows.

Continue to Loudonville and stop at Creative Outlet where you'll find Indian items, handmade jewelry, and Australian Outback coats. If you head south on State 3 and turn left on County Road 23, you'll come to the Mohican River

Inn, a weekender favorite. Mohican State Park, west of Loudonville on State 39, and Mohican Memorial State Forest, south of town on State 39 and west on State 97, are both well worth a visit.

State 97 continues through the highlands along the Clear Fork River into Lexington. From here, you can either continue your holiday at the Clear Fork Reservoir or hop on I-71 for a quick return to Cleveland or Columbus.

For More Information

Berlin Visitors Bureau: 330-893-3467

Holmes County Chamber of Commerce and Tourism Bureau: 330-674-3975

Loudonville-Mohican Tourist Information: 419-994-5225 or 800-722-7588

Victorian House (Millersburg): 330-674-1576 or 330-674-6761

Rastetter Woolen Mill (Millersburg): 330-674-2103

Bigham House Bed and Breakfast, 151 South Washington Street (Millersburg): 330-674-2337

The White House (Millersburg): 330-674-4311

Dutch Country Kitchen (Berlin): 330-893-4142

Mennonite Information Center: 330-893-3192

Berlin Bulk Foods (Berlin): 330-893-2353

Amish Farm (Berlin): 330-893-3232

Dutch Harvest (Berlin): 330-893-3333

Winesburg Craft House (Winesburg): 330-359-5599

Alpine-Alpa (Wilmot): 330-359-5454

Yoder's Amish Home (between Trail and Walnut Creek):
330-893-2541

Der Dutchman (Walnut Creek): 330-893-2981

Carlisle House (Walnut Creek): 330-893-2535

Holmes County Flea Market (Walnut Creek): 330-893-2836

Swiss Hat (Sugarcreek): 330-852-2821

Countryview Inn (Charm): 330-893-3003

Chalet in the Valley (Charm): 330-893-2550

Killbuck Valley Museum (Killbuck): 330-276-7381 or
330-276-8025

Bittersweet Farm (Killbuck): 330-276-1977

Mohican River Inn (Loudonville): 800-228-5118

5

Wandering Wayne County

Getting there: Interstates have, perhaps mercifully, bypassed most of Wayne County, whose core city is Wooster. I-71, which runs from Cleveland to Columbus, cuts across the northwest corner of the county. Wooster is 50 miles south of Cleveland, 100 miles northeast of Columbus, and 30 miles southwest of Akron.

Highlights: Wooster College, quaint Amish settlements, a four-season feast of nature's sights and scents.

Named for General "Mad" Anthony Wayne, whose name is encountered often in Ohio rambles, this lovely county of rolling hills and patchwork farm fields was long roamed by Wyandotte and Delaware Indians before the first white men came. One of them was John Chapman, whose nursery along Little Sugar Creek produced apple seedlings, some of which probably ended up in the orchard of Delaware chief Beaver Hat, whose cabin overlooked Apple Creek.

The legacy of Chapman, now known as Johnny Appleseed, lives on, not just in the area's beloved apple trees but in the 2,000-acre Ohio Agricultural Research and Development Center (OARDC), the largest research institute of its kind in the nation. The county is a rich producer of dairy products, wheat, corn, and potatoes.

This is a good place to start a tour. Heading south from Wooster on State 83, turn left into the OARDC just south of the U.S. 30 interchange. The grounds are open daily, and there is no "off" season here. Wander through forests of rhododendron, alleys of flowering crab apple, seas of azaleas, and three acres of bright rose gardens. The Secrest Arboretum is one of the country's finest. Admission to OARDC is free.

The first Amish settlers came to this area after 1817, and the "plain people" still play an important part in area tourism. Their largest concentration in Ohio is in Wayne and Holmes Counties.

Turning southeast on U.S. 250 to Apple Creek, watch for the old post office building in the center of town, now Hearts and Flowers, which sells handicrafts and Amish dolls. When the road makes a big bend, watch for Troyer's Home Pantry at 668 West Main Street—an Amish bakery and dining room, as well known for its take-home pie shells as it is for its eat-in angel food cakes, custard pies, and pillow-sized cinnamon rolls. Staying on U.S. 250, a mile east of town, stop at Red Barn Furniture to see handcrafted Amish cabinetry for indoors and out. Among their popular items are old-fashioned lawn gliders and porch swings. The shop, which also does "bespoke" work (furniture made to order), is closed Sunday.

Turn left on County 79 to Kidron, where, just north of town on County 52, the Ohio Mennonite Relief Sale and Quilt Auction is held each year on the first Saturday in August at Central Christian School. To quilt-lovers, it's an event of international importance, with more than 100 handmade quilts auctioned off. In addition, booths sell everything from noodles to grandfather clocks, and pies to handmade furniture.

Whether or not you're here for the one big sale day, Kidron is worth a long look. A mile north of County 79, also on County 52, furniture fanciers will want to stop at The Nut Tree, where craftsmen make home and office furniture using dovetail, dowel, and mortise-and-tenon construction. Orders are taken for your choice of style, wood, and finish.

The Town and Country Store Restaurant at 4959 Kidron Road (County 52) offers traditional rural Amish dining at its most authentic, but is open only for breakfast and lunch: midday is the big mealtime in this hardworking farm country. The restaurant stays open until 5:00 P.M. on Thursday.

The livestock auction held every Thursday at 11:00 A.M. in downtown Kidron is a folk event not to be missed. Even when you don't understand what's going on in the auction arena, there are plenty of other things going on, including parades of cute kids, lambs, and piglets, and a lively flea market. Farm-fresh produce is sold here, and special events and sales are sometimes scheduled too, so call the Visitors and Convention Bureau at 330-264-1800 or 800-362-6474 to ask if anything is afoot during the time you'll be in the area.

One of the biggest tourist attractions is—believe it or not—a hardware store. Because the Amish live simply and without electricity, Lehman's Hardware at 4779 Kidron Road carries the state's largest selection of wood stoves, gas refrigerators, hand tools, and other gadgets that require no household power.

For a century, the little crossroads village has been a shopping center for the Amish. It still is, despite the stream of curious tourists. The old flour mill, a relic of the 1930s, next to Lehman's Hardware is a shopping center for handicrafts from local artisans as well as crafts from 35 developing nations worldwide.

From the Kidron area, continue east on County 79, then take State 94 north through Amish farm country to Dalton, where the Village Antique Mall houses 15 dealers selling everything from books to quilts. Turn left (west) on U.S. 30, and follow it to Das Dutch Kitchen, a 130-year-old Victorian home turned restaurant at 14278 Lincoln Way East. Dine in, then stop at the gift shop and bakery.

Continue west on U.S. 30 and, if antiques are your passion, stop just east of State 57 at Black Cat Antiques, an eclectic blend of furniture, stoneware, quilts, baskets, and collectibles. Turning right on State 57 brings you past the Simply Smucker's Store and into Orrville, where delicious fruity smells come from Smucker's plant, whose jams and jellies are sold nationwide.

If you keep heading west on U.S. 30, you'll return to Wooster. Just past the intersection of State 94A, stop at Johnny's Swiss Country Store. It's stocked with Amish cheeses, trail bologna, baked goods, dried fruits, and souvenirs.

If you're not yet ready to return to Wooster, jog north at Honeytown on County 54 for a look at Smithville. The Smithville Inn on the town square was built as a stagecoach stop in 1818. Today it's a family restaurant known for its pies, billowy biscuits, and chicken. Just south on 585 is the popular barn restautant and the shops of Buchanan Place.

Save at least several hours for the College of Wooster, founded in 1866. Its campus could be a movie set, with its dignified old buildings and stunning state-of-the-art new ones.

Although the Wooster Inn dates only to 1959, its Georgian Colonial style fits right into the traditional campus. Guests have included Robert Frost, Cathy Rigby, and Vincent Price, not to mention the hordes of proud alumnae who return time and again. A Mobil three-star restaurant, the Wooster Inn also has 16 comfortable rooms.

While in town, visit the Wayne County Historical Society Museum at 546 East Bowman Street, which exhibits historical objects from Indian times through the turn of the century. There's also a log cabin and old schoolhouse. The museum is closed Monday and holidays.

If you're ready now for a break from country roads, linger in the revitalized downtown for the many unique specialty shops, an Everything Rubbermaid store, and a Corning Revere Factory store.

For More Information

Wayne County Visitors and Convention Bureau (Wooster):
330-264-1800 or 800-362-6474

Ohio Agricultural Research and Development Center (OARDC):
330-263-3779

College of Wooster: 330-263-2000

Wooster Inn: 330-264-2341

Wayne County Historical Society Museum (Wooster):
330-264-8856

6

In Defiance

Getting there: Defiance is 60 miles southwest of Toledo and about 110 miles north of Dayton.

Highlights: The Maumee and Auglaize Rivers, historic AuGlaize Village.

When the Harley-Davidson motorcycle company singled out the 18-mile stretch of State 424 between Defiance and Napoleon as one of the 10 best touring roads in the United States, it caught our attention. Actually, most of the route along the Maumee River, starting at the U.S. 24 exit off I-475 and ending at the Indiana border, is a delightful country drive sought out for its scenery.

Meander bonny banks lined with cottonwood, locust, beech, and ash trees, and drive through stretches of farm fields, meadows, and orchards. In higher country along the limestone ridges, butternut and black walnut reign.

U.S. 24 takes you out of Toledo in a southwesterly direction. If you want to take a sightseeing ride on the Bluebird Passenger Train, which runs between Waterville and Grand Rapids (weekends and holidays from mid-May through October, Tuesday and Thursday in July and August), call ahead to get schedules and reservations.

Once you get to Grand Rapids, check out the old Isaac Ludwig Mill in Providence Park, which is open from May to October. Call ahead. Demonstrations are free, but schedules vary.

Floods have always been a curse in this area, but they are also a part of the Maumee River's rich history. As late as 1959, downtown Grand Rapids filled in five minutes. The top of the mill served as a refuge for those who were caught in the lowlands. In the park, which is on the north side of the river, you can also catch the Shawnee Princess paddlewheeler, an authentic steamboat that offers sightseeing cruises on the Maumee.

The information center in Grand Rapids is housed in a log cabin on Front Street at the railroad bridge. Stop for the latest information and maps, then drive down Front Street (State 65), with its colorful shops and restaurants. This was once two cities—Providence on the north side of the river, Gilead on the south—but it all became Grand Rapids in time.

Traveling west on State 65, stop to picnic or walk the old canal towpath at Mary Jane Thurston State Park. Continue picking up State 110, which takes you into Napoleon. From there, get on State 424, which follows the river, using the old towpath of the Miami-Erie and Wabash-Erie canal systems. Their completion was one of the most exciting eras in Ohio history. For a heady few decades at the height of the canals' heyday, people could travel by boat to Toledo, Fort Wayne, Dayton, and even Cincinnati.

You'll see a section of the Miami and Erie Canal, still filled with water, at Independence Dam State Park. In the segment is one lock; a three-mile hiking path follows the canal. The park has camping, fishing above and below the dam, and picnic tables.

The original wood locks at Defiance were slow, allowing plenty of time for thirsty crews to take shore leave in local

taverns. Business boomed as commercial travelers came
went, and farmers brought their hogs and harvests to town
for shipment out on the canals. Even after the railroad
arrived, the canals flowed on for a time, carrying logs and
other bulk freight.

The route has been a canoe course and footpath since the
first humans inhabited Ohio. The confluence of the Auglaize
and Maumee Rivers was a natural meeting point for Indian
tribes. Chief Pontiac was born here. Huge tribal councils con-
vened on the rivers, and blood-curdling attacks, kidnappings,
and battles beset the early white settlers.

It was here that General "Mad" Anthony Wayne, the
hero of Ticonderoga and Stony Point, faced down the British
and their Indian allies at the famous Battle of Fallen Timbers
and won Ohio forever. Had the tide of battle turned differ-
ently, Ohio could be a part of Canada today.

The earliest white settlers found that much of the region
was covered in a wasteland they called the Great Black
Swamp. Wild wolves roamed in packs. Mosquitoes swarmed
in thick, stinging clouds. Poisonous snakes were poised to
strike the unwary. A historian wrote in 1846 that "when it is
drained and cleared it will be the garden of Ohio." That it is.
The largest Campbell soup factory in the world is now here,
close to the lush harvests.

It was the flood of 1913 that ended the canal era. Two of
the locks can still be seen in town, one from South Jackson
Street and the other from Terrawanda Drive. The old lock-
keeper's house from South Jackson is now a part of AuGlaize
Village.

Coming into Defiance from the east on State 424, cross the
river on State 66 and turn left on Fort Street, to the point
where the Auglaize and Maumee meet. This is the site of the
original fort and a focal point for the historic downtown area.

An heir to the tradition of canal town hospitality is
Kissner's Tavern-Restaurant downtown at Fifth and Clinton.

It has been family owned and operated since 1928.
Stop in for breakfast, lunch, or dinner and for a look
at the elegant, original cherry and mahogany back
bar. Historic downtown Defiance is the revitalized
center of town, with its colorful shops and regal
courthouse.

Leaving town by heading west on State 424,
you'll pass through a vibrant chronicle of American
architecture starting with splendid Victorian styles—
Greek Revival, Italianate, and Queen Anne—followed
by newer designs—the Prairie school, Sears Roebuck kit
homes, and the bungalow.

Roll on through the river scenery along the Auglaize on
State 111. You'll also have a view of the dam, which has been
running electrical generators since 1912. A mile before you
reach Junction, there's a roadside rest area, which is a good
spot to enjoy the view and stretch your legs.

Between 1811 and 1828, Johnny Appleseed operated some
of his biggest nurseries along the north bank of the Maumee,
opposite the mouth of the Auglaize. Driving these roads, you
see acres of orchards, many of them descendants of the thousands of seedlings he started here.

Johnny planted other things, too. Known to the Indians
as a medicine man because of his talents with herbs, he
planted mint, garlic, pennyroyal, and other healing herbs
along the Maumee, Auglaize, Tiffin, and smaller streams that
thread this area. If you stumble across a patch of wild mint or
a field of buttery dandelions, it could be that their ancestors
were put there by Johnny himself.

Truly a beehive of history-come-alive, the AuGlaize Village
Farm Museum re-creates the rural Ohio of the 19th century.
The red barn on the grounds is original, and houses a

museum. Other buildings are authentic, moved here from other sites, or are faithful replicas.

The village is complete, from the sawmill to a smoke-house, post office, and general store. There's almost always something special going on—apple-butter boiling, molasses-making, old-fashioned yule, Civil War reenactment, or an old-time car show. During special events, costumed personnel perform their work as though they were living 150 years ago. There is an admission fee for the village.

An additional (or alternate) side trip is to head northwest out of Defiance on State 15 for about eight miles to the Oxbow Lake Wildlife Area. Hunting and fishing around the 45-acre lake and in the 371 acres of woods and fields are legendary.

Leaving the Defiance area, head north on State 66 for about 22 miles. Just past Archbold, turn right on State 2. Sauder Farm and Craft Village is a living-history complex that takes about three hours to explore thoroughly. You're welcome to stay all day for the price, immersing yourself in the sights and scents of a northern Ohio of yesteryear.

Dine in the Barn Restaurant under hand-hewn timbers, shop for quilts and crafts, watch artisans at their daily tasks, or come for special events in the air-conditioned Founder's Hall. The village is open every day from late April until November 1; the shops are open year-round.

You may wish to take a trip on the *Arawanna Belle,* an authentic sternwheeler that plies the Maumee River out of Toledo on lunch, dinner, moonlight, and entertainment cruises of varying lengths. Call 419-691-7447.

You're now about halfway between exits 2 and 3 of the Ohio Turnpike (I-80/I-90), and the quickest route to points east and west.

For More Information

Chamber of Commerce (Defiance): 419-782-7946 or
   800-686-4382, E-mail: tourism@defiance=online.com

Bluebird Passenger Train: 419-878-2177

Isaac Ludwig Mill (Grand Rapids): 419-832-8932

Independence Dam State Park: 419-784-3263

Kissner's Tavern-Restaurant (Defiance): 419-782-1116

AuGlaize Village: 419-784-0107 or 419-782-7255

Sauder Farm and Craft Village (including the Barn Restaurant):
   419-445-9610 or 800-590-9755

7

The Lake Erie Islands

Getting there: Port Clinton is 208 miles from Cincinnati, 68 miles from Cleveland, and 175 miles from Dayton.

Highlights: Remote, windswept, alluring, and aloof islands with an air of romantic yesteryear; a haven for campers, fishermen, and hideaway seekers of all kinds.

Some of the best country roads in Ohio are roads you may choose *not* to drive in your own car. The islands are reached by ferry or air; parking for your car is provided at ferry docks or airports. Although you can take your car to Kelleys Island or Put-in-Bay on ferries, all the islands are best traveled on foot, by bicycle or golf cart, or on a commercial tour. (On South Bass Island, you can also rent an antique car by the hour or day.) Unless you'll be staying more than a few days, it's cheaper and far less encumbering to manage without transporting your car.

Kelleys Island

The entire Kelleys Island is on the National Register of Historic Places and is a mecca for photographers, shipwreck divers, and cruising boaters, not to mention many avid fishermen. Reach the island by a 20-minute ferry ride from Marblehead (State 163, north of Sandusky Bay) or on the hour-long ferry from Sandusky. Ferry service is also run from Kelleys Island to Cedar Point. Airline service is from Sandusky and Port Clinton.

Originally settled by Paleo-Indians as early as 12,000 B.C., the island entered the modern age in the 1830s when a limestone quarry was opened. Majestic Greek Revival, Gothic, Queen Anne, and Italianate homes, many of them built of native stone, dot the island. Some quarrying is still done today, and the island's second industry, winemaking, continues to thrive as well.

The best place to start a tour is at the Chamber of Commerce Information Center along the lakeshore near Division Street. Nothing on the island is more than a brief bicycle ride away—the island is only five miles wide—so ask for guidance and maps depending on whether you want to go to the beach, hike through old quarries with their carpets of wildflowers, or pedal around the island rubbernecking.

Clustered downtown are shops, bars, restaurants, fishing charters, and places where you can rent a bicycle, cart, or moped. It's the heart of the island's tourist business. A short walk or bike ride up Division takes you to Chapel Street, where you'll find the island's two stately old churches, then turn right on Addison past the pavilion and ballpark and back to Lakeshore Drive, where the original Kelley Mansion stands. It's privately owned, but sporadic tours are available. Ask about them while you're here. A three-story mansion built of native fieldstone, the home has a stunning "floating" staircase, bathed in rosy light from a skylight made of red glass.

Across the street is Inscription Rock with its ancient Indian pictographs. Although erosion has erased much of the detail of the original drawings, someone had the foresight in 1850 to sketch them and they have been reproduced. Admission is free.

Continuing out Woodford Road for about half a mile,

look for the Kelleys Island Wine Company on your right. A 6,000-square-foot pavilion is open for dining from an extensive menu. Tastings are offered in a farmhouse dating to the Civil War era. It's open daily in season, weekends in shoulder season, and other times by appointment. Tour the winery, get a picnic lunch from the gourmet deli, and enjoy the brilliant, breezy gardens.

A sandy beach spreads along the northern shore of the island less than two miles out Division Street. If it's time for a meal, stop at Fresch's Island House, a block north of the docks on Division Street. Open daily in season for breakfast, lunch, and dinner, it serves continental favorites in a gracious old homestead.

Continuing your route, you'll pass the Sweet Valley Inn on your left. A Victorian relic, it is furnished with period antiques and offers its guests carriage rides in the evening.

Turn right at the lake to the beach and state park (standard state park admissions are charged), and go left for a look at the impressive glacial grooves. They tell a dramatic story of the shaping of this area by the grinding of giant glaciers some 30,000 years ago, forming one of the longest and most dramatic glacial grooves in North America. Outdoor exhibits explain what happened; admission is free. Return to the harbor on Division Street.

A leisurely pedal west from the docks on Water Street takes you past some of the island's finest old mansions, some of them now bed-and-breakfasts. Zettler's Lakeview Bed and Breakfast is a Victorian home whose front parlor overlooks the lake. The Inn on Kelleys Island was built in 1876, has a private beach, and is loaded with antiques.

Put-in-Bay

Located on South Bass Island, this historic harbor has all the elements for a yachting picture book. Billowing sails, foamy

Perry's Victory and International Peace Memorial, Put-in-Bay

wakes, the fizz and bustle of passing boats, a sprawling park, and a turn-of-the-century yacht club add to the local color, offering enjoyment for landlubbers as well as for flocks of yachties and fisherfolk.

Ferries serve Put-in-Bay from Catawba Point, which lies at the end of State 53 North, and from downtown Port Clinton. Griffing Flying Service provides air transportation to the island from Sandusky and Port Clinton. A ferry also runs from

Cedar Point to Put-in-Bay on Monday. Take exit 6 or 7 from I-80 or I-90, or drive the lakeshore along State 2. The voyage is about three miles; the flight is about 10 minutes.

Well before landing you'll see Perry's Victory and International Peace Memorial, which dominates the view, soaring more than 300 feet above the lake. Said to be the largest Doric column in the world, the monument is a massive 45 feet in diameter.

Operated by the National Park Service from early May until late October, the 25-acre park commemorates the victory of Commodore Oliver Hazard Perry and his fleet of nine American boats over a powerful British flotilla during the War of 1812.

It was a turning point in the war, allowing Perry's ships to take American troops to the Canadian mainland, defeat the redcoats at the Battle of the Thames River, and put a permanent end to the threats of British and Indian intrusions into the U.S. side of Lake Erie.

Take the elevator to the top of the monument, where the lake views are second only to those from airplanes. Adults pay a small admission charge at the monument; children and senior citizens enter free. An additional fee is charged for taking the elevator. The monument is open daily from 10:00 A.M. to 5:00 P.M. in spring and fall, 9:00 A.M. to 6:00 P.M. in summer.

Bicycle rentals are available both at the Lime Kiln docks and at Put-in-Bay. A suggested route for a one-day bicycle tour is to start at the docks in Put-in-Bay. Go south on Catawba Avenue, east on Delaware (where you can ride the delightful 1917 carousel), then north on Toledo. Harbour Square, on the corner of Toledo and Delaware, is a quaint shopping complex. Across from it is the bus depot. Head back up Toledo to Bayview, where you turn right to get to Perry's Monument.

When you return to the island's shopping and dining district, you'll have a large choice of burgers, ice cream parlors, candy shops, baked foods, pizza, tacos, subs, seafood, and saloons. Most visitors like to stroll from spot to spot, stopping to have a glass of wine here, a snack there, and browse the boutiques in between.

If the day is hot and you want a sit-down meal, try the perch platter at the Boat House, where there's live entertainment on weekends, or the Crescent Tavern, known for its smoked ribs and house wines. For dancing, there's the Round House Bar; for the longest bar in the world—150 stools—go to the Beer Barrel Saloon. Tipper's has seafood and steaks. The Crew's Nest is a private club, but you can buy a membership for the day or weekend.

Rather than concentrate on a specific spot, if you're in the mood to tipple or nosh, it's more fun to stroll the streets, following the scents and sounds to an uncrowded niche (or the kind of crowd you want). Also downtown is Kimberly's Carousel, a merry-go-round built in 1917 and still in merry condition. Hop on one of the delightful, carved creatures and you're a kid again.

After leaving the monument, head south on Toledo to Langram Road, and watch for Stonehenge on your right. Built of locally quarried dolomite, the house and old wine-pressing cottage are open on summer days for tours. Admission is charged for adults; children accompanied by an adult are free. The gift shop features nautical antiques.

Pass the airstrip and continue a mile to the Lime Kiln docks. If you're on foot, you can catch a bus from here back to Put-in-Bay. The lighthouse beyond the docks isn't open to the public, but it makes a good backdrop for the camera.

Retracing your route on Langram, follow signs that direct a left turn on the Bicycle Route. Stop at Maple Leaf Cemetery—gravestones always tell an eloquent story of an area's past—then turn right on Put-in-Bay Road and left on Meechen Road, which takes you into the state park. Here you can camp, picnic, swim off the beach, or seek out the ruins of the Hotel Victory, an enormous wooden hotel that burned early in the century. In its heyday the Victory, which billed itself as the largest summer hotel in the world, hosted hordes of visitors from Detroit, Sandusky, Cleveland, and Toledo on steamboats.

Return to Put-in-Bay by heading east on Catawba Avenue, which takes you by Crown Hill Cemetery. If you follow West Shore Boulevard to the lake, you'll come upon the startling sight of a ship nestled in the cliffs overlooking Victory Cove. Once Henry Ford's flagship, the grounded vessel now called The Boat House has a dining room where top entertainers perform in season. Call ahead to see who is playing.

Back on Catawba Avenue, stop at two caves: Perry's Cave, which echoes with legends and rumors, was where Admiral Perry stored munitions and later, 52 feet below the surface, housed prisoners of war. Crystal Cave, calling itself the world's largest geode, is a wonderland of sparkle. It's on the grounds of the Heineman Winery, founded in 1886. One modest admission price covers the winery tour, tasting, and the cave.

Catawba Avenue returns you to the docks. From here, a ferry can take you to Middle Bass Island. If you want to stay, the 50-room Parker's Inn in downtown Put-in-Bay is a hotel with a fine restaurant and gift shops. The full-service restaurant serves everything from burgers to gourmet meals, and the location is perfect for walking to downtown shopping, dining, pub-crawling, and good times. Facing the park is the Park Hotel, a traditional favorite, with cozy rooms and pleasant staff.

Other Islands

Middle Bass Island, home of the historic Lonz Winery, can be reached by air from Port Clinton or Sandusky, by water taxi from downtown Put-in-Bay at the boardwalk, or by Miller's

Ferry from Catawba Point. Listed on the National Register of Historic Places, the winery is a favorite fun spot for boat owners who come here for picnics, the weekend entertainment, or the Grape Festival in September. Tour the winery, taste the unique wines, shop the nautical gift shop, and sample the Lonz snack bar's famous pizza.

Pelee Island is actually in Canada, but it's an important jewel in this cluster of Lake Erie islands. Part of the fun in visiting here is to cross an international border with its pleasant, but necessary, formalities. It's a two-hour ferry ride from Sandusky; air transportation is from Sandusky and Port Clinton. A 10,000-acre preserve, it is the scene of a lively pheasant hunt each fall, sportfishing in summer and ice fishing in winter, and excellent bird-watching.

The island is mostly undeveloped. Its few amenities are located near the West Dock. There is also a winery with a pavilion for tastings. An alternate way to view Pelee is aboard the Pelee Island Ferry, which sails several times a week from Sandusky to Leamington, Ontario, home of the largest tomato processing plant in the world. The passage includes a visit to Point Pelee National Park, a bird sanctuary, tropical gardens, art galleries, and dozens of shops.

For More Information

Erie County Visitors and Convention Bureau: 419-625-2984 or 800-255-ERIE, Website: www.Buckeyenorth.com

Ottawa County Visitors Bureau: 419-734-4FUN or 800-441-1271

Kelleys Island Chamber of Commerce: 419-746-2360, Website: www.KelleysIsland.com

Kelleys Island Wine Company: 419-746-2537

Fresch's Island House (Kelleys Island): 419-746-2304

The Village Pump (Kelleys Island): 419-746-2281

Toy Museum (Kelleys Island): 419-746-2451

Butterfly Box (Kelleys Island): 419-746-2454

Put-in-Bay Chamber of Commerce: 419-285-2832,
   E-mail: www.Put-In-Bay.com

Crescent Tavern (Put-in-Bay): 419-285-4211

Crew's Nest (Put-in-Bay): 419-285-3625

Kimberly's Carousel (Put-in-Bay): 419-285-2832

The Boat House (Put-in-Bay): 419-285-5665

The Lunt House (Put-in-Bay): 419-285-2585

Parker's Inn (Put-in-Bay): 419-285-5555

Park Hotel (Put-in-Bay): 419-285-3581

Tipper's (Put-in-Bay): 419-285-TIPS

Bird's Nest Resort (South Bass Island): 419-285-6119 or
   419-693-8628

Pelee Island Pheasant Farm (hunt information): 419-724-2931

Mill Point Lodge Country Inn (Pelee Island): 519-724-2223 or
   519-326-9837

Stonehill Bed and Breakfast (Pelee Island): 519-724-2193

Twin Oaks Bed and Breakfast (Pelee Island): 800-661-2220

8

Sandusky and Erie County

Getting there: Sandusky is 224 miles from Cincinnati, 63 miles from Cleveland, 117 miles from Columbus, and 171 miles from Dayton.

Highlights: Historic Cedar Point, country roads and farm markets, railroad history, and Thomas A. Edison's boyhood home.

If you're following the Lake Erie Circle Tour, which travels the entire lip of Ohio from the Pennsylvania line across northern Ohio and back via Canada, Erie County offers some of the best detours and diversions along the route. One is the chance to jump off to tour the islands, which are covered in Chapter 7. The other is the drive out a long finger of sandspit to the remote outpost of Cedar Point.

Our route takes us west out of Cleveland. Two miles east of Huron on U.S. 6, you'll pass the Old Woman Creek National Estuarine Reserve, where the visitors center is open Wednesday through Sunday. Hiking trails are open every day. Because it is one of the best of the Midwest's remaining undeveloped coastal wetlands areas and because we are beginning to understand how crucial are these swampy areas, once thought to be wastelands, a visit here is entertaining as well as educational.

Continue west on U.S. 6 through Huron. Just past Sheldon Marsh State Nature Preserve on your right and Camp Road on your left, turn right on the Cedar Point Chaussee. It's like driving out to sea as you probe farther and farther out into the lake on this narrow spit of land.

One of the oldest resorts in the nation, Cedar Point was once a summer playground for Clevelanders who traveled west by trolley car. Imagine gentlemen in their straw boaters and ladies in starched muslins, towing little girls with sausage curls and sons in sailor suits as they arrived for a summer holiday at the elegant Hotel Breakers.

In 1870 Cedar Point consisted of a dance floor and a boathouse on the beach. By the late 1870s, the resort had 16 bathhouses where guests could change into *rented* swimsuits! A water trapeze was built in the 1880s, beginning an era of thrill rides in which Cedar Point still excels. Its roller coasters consistently get top marks from the world's roller-coaster aficionados.

The first roller coaster was built here in 1892 and went only 10 miles per hour; today's screamers plummet 200 feet or more at speeds up to 65 miles an hour. Snake River Falls plunges passengers 80 feet into a basin, creating massive waves that drench and delight everyone in sight.

Football legend Knute Rockne got his start at Cedar Point as a lifeguard in 1913. Nellie Melba and Enrico Caruso sang here. Big bands, including Woody Herman's, Guy Lombardo's, and Benny Goodman's, played here in the coliseum. Abbot and Costello hosted a war bond drive here in 1942. Arsenio Hall worked at Cedar Point in the 1970s.

The 364-acre peninsula is one of the nation's premier playgrounds, with 60 rides, three antique carousels, one of the largest marinas on the lakes, a campground, sandy beach, go-cart course, suites hotel, and the timeless Hotel Breakers, with its stained-glass windows and wicker furniture.

A visit to Cedar Point is not a side trip to be taken lightly in a few rushed hours. Check in for as long as you can. If you're here just for the day, arrive early and plot your day carefully by studying show schedules and the park map. It is varied and enormous—truly worth a visit of a couple of days.

Many visitors beat the traffic tie-ups by taking a ferry from downtown Sandusky or from the islands. Cedar Point also makes a popular day trip for people who are staying on Kelleys Island or Put-in-Bay.

The theme park opens in May and closes in October, with more limited hours before Memorial Day and after Labor Day. Nearby hotels are open all year, but Cedar Point hotels open and close with the park. Call to inquire about marina and campground schedules.

Leave the peninsula on the Cedar Point Causeway, which delivers you back to U.S. 6 just east of downtown Sandusky. In both directions you'll find there is a good choice of accommodations including well-known chain motels.

If you decide to detour into Sandusky, a prime target should be the Merry-Go-Round Museum on U.S. 6 at the corner of Washington and Jackson Streets. While viewing one of the world's most important carousel collections, you can ride an indoor merry-go-round, listen to calliope music, and see all sorts of carousel memorabilia. There's also a carving shop where a modern workman makes classic merry-go-round masterpieces.

Only two blocks to the southeast, at Wayne Street and East Adams, is the Follett House Museum in a stately Greek Revival home that dates to the 1830s. A branch of the public library, it has no admission fee. Hours are limited and vary with the seasons, so call ahead. Of special interest are Civil War artifacts related to a prison camp for Confederate officers on Johnson's Island in Sandusky Bay.

If you want to see the island itself, it's reached via a toll causeway south of Marblehead. More than 9,000 Confederate soldiers passed through this area; 206 of them are buried here in the cold Yankee soil. Services on Memorial Day are particularly moving.

Also downtown is the Eleutheros Cooke House and Garden. The Greek Revival home is furnished with antiques and houses an impressive display of ruby and cranberry glass. Don't miss the gardens and greenhouse. From downtown, you can also take an Island Hopping Cruise to the islands or on a dinner-dance evening. Any time you're in the city, pay pilgrimage to Washington Park downtown with its Victorian-raised flowerbeds, floral clock, and famous Boy with the Boot fountain. It's considered one of the best public parks in Ohio.

Sandusky is a colorful harbor town offering offbeat shopping, historic homes, boating, and dining. Wagner's 1844 Inn is an Italianate home listed on the National Register of Historic Places. At the Tea Rose Tearoom next door, owner Ellen Kraus will read your leaves. The Red Gables is a stately Tudor-style home named for its scarlet-gabled exterior; the Cottage Rose is a 1913 Tudor-style home.

From U.S. 6, turn south on State 269, which brings you to Lagoon Deer Park, situated between U.S. 6 and State 2. More than 250 animals from around the globe are here for families to pet and feed. You can also fish in stocked lakes.

If you go south from Sandusky on State 4, also called Columbus Avenue and Wright Brothers Memorial Highway, you'll pass through an area of peaceful rural croplands and neat country homes.

Six miles south of the city, where State 4 crosses State 99 just north of the turnpike, stop at Gastier's Strawberry Hill Farm to stock up on Lake Erie wines, fresh local fruits and vegetables, and homemade German breads and pastries. On Route 6 on the west side of Sandusky, Firelands Winery is open for tours and tastings, and it has a gift shop where you'll want to linger.

Continue south six more miles, passing more country houses and patchwork farms, heading toward Bellevue, where you'll eventually turn east on State 113 and go through some of Ohio's prettiest farmland with hills, crossroads, and creek crossings.

In Bellevue itself, at 253 West Street, stop at the Mad River and NKP Railroad Society Museum, with its exhibits of Ohio rail memorabilia. On display are entire locomotives, cars, and cabooses, a postal car, a reefer car, and a diesel locomotive, as well as impressive collections of timetables, old photos, and souvenirs of a vanished era. Best of all, most of the volunteers who help out at the museum are railroad retirees who can answer almost any question you ask. The museum is open daily in summer and on weekends in shoulder seasons. There's no admission charge, but donations are put to good use. It's best to call ahead at 419-483-2222.

If you dip south on State 269 for three miles, then turn right two miles later on Thompson Township Road, you'll come to Seneca Caverns. A crack in the earth that has drawn curious visitors since 1872, this phenomenon allows you to explore 147 feet below ground level. You'll pass through many levels and several rooms on your way to the river at the bottom.

Guided tours take an hour. Bring a warm sweater because the temperature in the depths stays in the 50s even on the hottest summer days. There are picnic tables on the grounds, and a place where you can pan for gemstones. The caverns are open daily in summer and on weekends in spring and fall; closed in winter.

Retrace your route back to State 113 and turn east for two miles. Historic Lyme Village is a complete working village of homes and outbuildings centered around a mansion (circa

1880), which now houses a museum. You'll see people going about their daily lives just as they might have done a century ago. Although the buildings are authentic, some were moved here from other places. One, a log cabin from Seneca County, was occupied by its owner from 1869 until she died in the early 1950s. The Seymour House, moved here in 1976 from a farm across the road, was built in 1836 and is thought to have been a stop on the Underground Railroad.

Historic Lyme Village is a complete time warp that the entire family will enjoy doubly during special events such as the Pioneer Days in mid-September and Christmas of Yesteryear in early December. It is open afternoons except Monday in-season and Sunday in May and September. Admission is charged, but children under age 12 are admitted free with adults.

Continue traveling east on U.S. 113 through uncrowded countryside, along what is known as the Edison Highway. This brings you to Milan, a prim and lovely community founded in 1817, which still shows the architectural legacy of its prosperous early settlers. After 1839, when a canal linked Milan to the lake, the village became one of the busiest and richest grain-shipping hubs on the Great Lakes.

Start at the village square, where there is a statue of the young Edison and his mother. The old city's center square, with its treasury of century-old buildings, is one of the state's finest. Well-preserved buildings now serve as shops, especially for antiques.

The Milan Inn at 29 East Church Street is a stagecoach stop that dates to the 1840s. Find some excuse to dine here, if only to see the murals showing the area's history. Closed Monday, the inn is open weekdays for lunch and dinner; on weekends, it's open for breakfast, too.

Following signs, turn north on Edison Drive to the Edison complex. Thomas A. Edison was born here in 1847 and lived with his parents in this pleasant brick homestead until he was seven. In 1906, he returned to buy the house from his sister's heirs, and electrified it with Edison lights in 1923. The home is near the Milan Historical Museum, noted for its doll and glass collections; an arts building where antiques and needle arts are on display; and the Sayles House, which was built a century ago and has been meticulously restored. Modest admission is charged for the Edison Home. The Milan Historical Museum accepts donations.

A half mile southeast of Milan on Edison Drive lies the Calpin Memorial Sanctuary, where you can walk marked paths through woodlands and wildflowers. Open daily, it makes a placid place to stretch your legs after a long drive. There is no admission fee.

Or you may want to shoot north on U.S. 250, where Poling's Peddlers Village has dozens of shops selling everything from diamonds to teddy bears, gifts, and arts under one roof. Have tea or a light lunch in the Victorian tearoom. Homestead Farms, at the Ohio Turnpike exit 7, is an inn and restaurant featuring the original home's 1883 marble fireplace.

If instead you continue east on U.S. 113, the road rises and falls with the gentle dance of rolling farmlands. Neat farms line the route, many of them selling whatever crop is abundant at the time. In springtime, load up on tender lettuces and sheaves of spring onions. From mid- to late summer, sweet corn is sold mere minutes after picking. The taste and bursting pop of its juices on the tongue are unforgettable. Fall turns the foliage bronze and the sky a deep blue as pumpkins and gourds pile onto farm-stand shelves. In winter, snow piles delicately on fencerows and covers the corn stubble.

Looking off to your right after Berlinville, the highest hill you see is 890 feet, the highest point in the county.

Nearing Birmingham, slow down so you don't miss two stores at the intersection of U.S. 113 & State 60. The Country Craft Store on your left and the Little Red Gift House on the right, with their homey harvest of Ohio treasures and collectibles, are the kinds of finds that make back-roads travel even more of a joy.

Turn right just past the Little Red Gift House to enter Schoeple Garden, a 70-acre botanical showplace. It's not staffed or well marked, but is a pleasant place to stroll and savor in any season. Some 400 floral species abound, and 500 rosebushes form a dazzling rose garden.

If you want to take a side trip into Oberlin, it's only a couple of miles south of State 113 on State 58. Stately and historic Oberlin College is on County 511. Stop at the admissions office in the Carnegie Building to ask about a guided or self-guided tour.

Points of interest on campus include the Allen Memorial Arts Museum, best known for its European and Japanese collections, and the biology museum in the Kettering Hall of Science. If you don't have time for the museums, it's a treat just to amble around the campus, lost in nostalgia and listening to scraps of music floating out of practice houses and rehearsal halls.

Founded in 1866 by Presbyterians and now independent, Oberlin was the first college in America to offer equal degrees to women and men, and to people of all races. Although most of the buildings have been built since 1964, the campus still has a feeling of heritage and history.

Returning north on State 58 brings you back to State 113, and a right turn leads to Elyria. Founded in 1811 and still the home of some fine old mansions, Elyria is a busy industrial center and county seat, but is worth penetrating for two points of interest. Right in the center of town, Cascade and Elywood parks offer verdant walking paths through waterfalls and cliffy rock formations. In winter, people assemble here to sled the hills; in summer, the sun-dappled playgrounds are a good spot for children to work off pent-up energy after a long ride.

The Hickories Museum at 509 Washington Avenue has interesting exhibits related to the history of Lorain County. It is open daily except Saturday and a small admission is charged. Or, just drive by it for a view of another of Ohio's magnificent mansions. This one was built in Tudor style in 1894.

Elyria brings you back to the western edge of the Cleveland metropolis at a spot where you can hop easily on the Ohio Turnpike or the interstates to start you on the fastest route home.

For More Information

Erie County Visitors and Convention Bureau: 419-625-2984 or 800-255-ERIE, Website: www.Buckeyenorth.com

Old Woman Creek National Estuarine Reserve (east of Huron): 419-433-4601

Cedar Point: 419-627-2350

Merry-Go-Round Museum (Sandusky): 419-626-6111

Follett House Museum (Sandusky): 419-627-9608

Johnson's Island (off Marblehead Peninsula): 419-734-4386

Ottawa County tourism information: 800-441-1271

Island Hopping Cruises: 419-626-5557 or 800-876-1907

Lagoon Deer Park (Sandusky): 419-684-5701 or 419-684-5627

Firelands Winery: 419-625-5475 or 800-548-WINE

Mad River and NKP Railroad Society Museum (Bellevue): 419-483-2222

Seneca Caverns (Bellevue): 419-483-6711

Historic Lyme Village (Bellevue): 419-483-4949 or
    419-483-6052

The Milan Inn (Milan): 419-499-4604

Thomas Edison Birthplace (Milan): 419-499-2135

Milan Historical Museum (Milan): 419-499-2968

Poling's Peddlers Village: 419-627-0851

Homestead Inn Restaurant: 419-499-4271

Homestead Inn (Homestead Farms): 419-499-4955

The Hickories Museum (Elyria): 419-322-3341

9

Nookdom

Getting there: This tour covers country roads in Hamilton County between Cincinnati and the Indiana border, and parts of Butler County, which begins at the Cincinnati bypass, I-275. The drives out of Cincinnati are 70 to 140 miles, depending on detours and side trips.

Highlights: The Shady-Nook and a beloved old theater organ, Miami University and McGuffey readers, Hueston Woods, the antique shops of Miamitown, historic Hamilton, and a log cabin village.

You won't find Nookdom on the map. Overshadowed by Cincinnati and not quite allied with any regional tourism promotion group, a few merchants in this area decided to break away and market their own vacation kingdom called Nookdom.

Leave Cincinnati on a westward course on I-74 or I-275. Turn north on State 128 and head for Miamitown, where you can browse antique shops galore. At last count, there were 35.

The road plays tag along high, handsome banks of the Miami River. Now you see it, now you don't. Between glimpses of the river itself, the traveler can delight in the sights of woodlands of maple, ash, and elm. Farm fields are planted in corn, soybeans, and truck crops, which are offered at the many roadside stands along the day's route. Of special interest are the many varieties of tomatoes grown in the Miami Valley. Ask about them when you stop at a friendly farm.

As you turn west onto State 126, you'll see another antique mall on the corner. This winding, two-lane road takes you past the occasional old barn, an old German church dating to 1886 on the right, and a quaint structure on the left. Donated by John Evans in 1887, it appears to have been a neighborly gesture in which Evans built a watering trough for passing horses.

Continuing on State 126 through Shandon, rich in comfortable old architecture, note the 1803 Congregational Church on your right and another church, dated 1900, on your left. Fields of hay along this route glisten green in summer, but are especially beautiful in fall after the hay harvest, when round bales are piled in fields, giving a golden contrast to the bright reds and yellows that cover the knolls.

The town of Okeana, a crossroads, is little more than a bridge, a railroad track, and a few homes. Follow the woodsy and winding road for about four miles through cornfields being gleaned by crows, and watch for a left turn onto Bebb Park Lane. As you head for the Governor Bebb Preserve, stop for a shot of the covered bridge, which was built in 1850, moved here to dry land, and restored.

Suddenly you find yourself in a log cabin village exactly like the settlement established here early in the 19th century by Welshmen. One of them, William Bebb, who was born in one of these original log cabins, became the 19th governor of the state.

In summer, the village bustles with activity as "pioneers" go about their business. The forge is fired for the blacksmith, schoolhouse doors open, herbs ripen, the shop sells real goods, and visitors are welcome to eavesdrop and observe.

Take a picnic lunch to eat on the shady grounds. If you need facilities, they are clearly labeled Womenfolk and Menfolk. Also on the 174-acre grounds is a 12-site primitive campground.

The Governor Bebb Preserve is open Saturday and Sunday from 1:00 to 5:00 P.M., May to September.

Leaving the park, return to State 126 and turn west toward Scipio for less than a mile. Take a sharp right on Route 129 at the state line and follow for about three miles to a left turn onto State 732 toward Oxford.

If you want to venture even farther off the beaten path, turn right off State 732 onto Dunwoody a mile north of State 129, and, a mile after that, go left onto Garner Road. Here, in the area known as Bunker Hill, is the undeveloped Pater Park Wildlife Area. Its 34 acres are mostly used by hunters in season, and at press time there were no facilities. Within the preserve, however, you'll find the Bunker Hill Universalist Pioneer Cemetery, where burials include soldiers from the Revolutionary War, War of 1812, Mexican War, and Civil War.

Another departure from State 732 is to turn west on Springfield at the Reily crossroads, then right after about half a mile onto Indian Creek Road. Indian Creek Preserve covers 135 acres along the creek. Picnic, hike, or fish here, and explore the 1810 burial ground. Many of the area's earliest settlers rest here. The brick church dates to 1829.

Returning to State 732 puts you back on course. The road zigzags dizzily through tiny Reily, where you'll see some lovely old homes. Watch for a small park on your left, with a manmade waterfall. This is a good place to pull over for a coffee break or a stretch. The road dead-ends at Brookville Road, and a right turn takes you into Oxford.

Entering town, the road becomes Chestnut Street. The first left turn after Main Street is Oak, which brings you to the McGuffey Museum on your right, at the corner of Spring Street, and to Miami University. Find parking in the area, and start here on a walking tour of the campus, which Robert Frost called America's "prettiest." Founded in 1809, Miami University is also known as the Williamsburg of the Midwest. Write ahead for a map of the college grounds, which are dotted with stately old buildings and threaded with parks and nature trails.

Highlights include a replica 14th-century Norman chapel, a carillon tower, Peabody Hall dating to 1871, pleasant gardens, and ponds alight with swans. Don't miss the formal gardens even in winter because they are lined with evergreens. Year-round, the benches here invite students and visitors alike to bask in the quiet, far from the tensions of city and classroom.

The McGuffey Museum has the finest and most complete collection of McGuffey *Eclectic Readers* in the world, including at least one copy of every edition. Although the rarer volumes are reserved for scholars, the old revolving school table is set with books that visitors are welcome to read.

In the books, lessons in the three Rs are based on object lessons and morality stories that have become firmly rooted in the American psyche. Brotherly love, honesty, hard work, thrift, and other traits shine through pages that also teach reading, writing, and 'rithmetic lessons.

The house, which was home to William Holmes McGuffey for 10 years when he was a faculty member at the university, is furnished with period pieces and is open for tours. Museums, art galleries, collections, and an herbarium are open to the public, and tours can be arranged. Admission to the McGuffey Museum is free. Hours for all sites vary with the school year, so call ahead.

We can't let you leave Oxford without mentioning Lottie Moon. Remember that Oxford was only a two-day stagecoach ride from the Ohio River, which separated the North from the South during the Civil War. The Moons had come from Tennessee, and their loyalties remained with the Confederacy.

Lottie, a social butterfly who had been engaged to a dozen men at once and who had jilted at the altar Ambrose Burnside, who became the Union's General Burnside, was the war's most daring spy. She was caught but used her cunning to beat the hangman, and she lived on after the war to become a foreign correspondent for a New York newspaper during the Franco-Prussian War. Local old-timers love to recount her story. Just ask.

Leaving town on State 732, you'll travel on a gently hilly two-lane road through farm fields and woodlands, passing regal farms rimmed with miles of white fencing. Just north of Oxford at Corso Road, you'll see the Black Bridge, originally called Pugh's Mill Bridge. A 200-foot-long beauty, it was built over Four Mile Creek at a date long forgotten. After Pugh's Mill burned in 1885, people gradually began calling it the Black Bridge, both because the Black family lived nearby and because another, white bridge was a mile down the creek.

Two points of interest bring visitors to the countryside north of Oxford. The Pioneer Farm and House Museum at Brown and Doty roads is a typical farm of the mid–19th century, filled with farm implements and other memorabilia from Ohio's early farm days. It's especially enjoyable in early June, during an arts and crafts fair, and in mid-October, when apple-butter stirrings send spicy scents spilling into the chilly air. Open from Memorial Day through October, the farm has specific hours and special events, so call ahead. A donation is requested.

Just east of here near the crossroads called Morning Sun is Hueston Woods State Park, said to have more visitors annually than Yellowstone National Park. A full resort offering lodgings and an excellent restaurant, the park also offers golf, fishing, swimming, hiking paths, a children's program in-season, and a huge fireplace in its sunlit lobby. It's a good place to stay overnight, either in the campground or in a hotel-style room overlooking the lake. Cottages with cooking facilities are also available.

Returning to Oxford, pick up U.S. 27 southbound. About a half mile past town, watch for a park on the right where you can pull over for a stretch and a stroll. The route takes you through McGonigle and past fields of fleecy sheep and rolling hills, sparkling with thimble-size farm ponds.

Six miles south of Oxford finds you at one of Ohio's most nostalgic restaurants: Shady-Nook. There's never a night without music at this cozy, relaxed country restaurant. Fun for everyone, it is especially enjoyed by those over age 60, who remember the famous Moon River radio program, beamed at midnight each Saturday from WLW in Cincinnati.

Listeners to the 500,000-watt station got a clear signal throughout most of the eastern United States, and the program's fans, still loyal after half a century, come from far and wide. For many, a trip to Shady-Nook is a pilgrimage to hear the same theater organ that was played on the show.

Tapes of old 1930s and 1940s shows, which are sold at the restaurant, reveal that the program featured sleepy, smarmy organ music accompanied by languid prose and poetry. It was, as we were told by one woman who was in high school during the era, "Great music to neck to." To older listeners, it was a soothing, hypnotic, sleeping potion to calm nerves after a busy workweek. Don't confuse the program with the song "Moon River," which came much later.

Dine on hearty country favorites while being serenaded by the massive, historic organ. Sometimes there are sing-alongs. On Sunday, the music starts at noon.

From here, U.S. 27 takes you speedily back south across the Miami River and into the Cincinnati orbit where we started. If you have time, however, stop in Hamilton, which is a short detour to the east on State 129. Once a thriving industrial city on the Miami-Erie Canal and steeped in 19th-century charm, Hamilton boasts not one, but three walking tours. Write ahead to the Chamber of Commerce or stop at their office at 201 Dayton Street to pick up descriptive maps of the self-guided walks.

North of downtown, a nine-block area called the German Village was platted in 1796, and was the city's first commercial, social, and neighborhood center. The historical museum is here, but the village's chief treasure is the Lane-Hooven House at 319 North Third Street. Its octagonal design was popularized in the mid-1850s, when a noted phrenologist touted the psychological benefits of living in an eight-sided house. (Phrenology is a "science" that analyzes people by feeling the bumps on their heads.) Psycho-babble aside, the house is magnificent with its steeply peaked roof, arched windows, butternut and ash woodwork, jigsaw gingerbread, spiral staircase, and stunning stained glass. The style is known as Gothic Victorian Revival. The museum is open most weekdays, but call ahead. Admission is free.

The area between Buckeye and High Streets, bordered by the railroad on the west and State 4 on the east, is called the Dayton-Lane area. It too is filled with fine Victorian mansions, most of them privately owned and viewable only during a leisurely walking tour up one street and down the other.

Also worth walking is the area west of the Great Miami River known as Rossville. Once a separate community, its heyday was from the 1830s through the early 20th century. Because this side of the river didn't flood as badly as the Hamilton side, more buildings remain from the early days.

On the west edge of Hamilton and entered from 2200 Hancock Avenue, park district headquarters are housed in a home that was built in 1835. The grounds, a five-acre arboretum, are worth exploring any time of year.

Hamilton is a beautiful little city, so let's linger here to reflect on Ohio's golden age. It began as a military outpost in 1791, creating a safe haven from Indians for a trickle of pioneers and traders who dared the new frontier. The city now covers the old fort site along the Great Miami River, where streets march uphill: First, Second, Third, and so on.

The city's three historical districts, all of them on the National Register of Historic Places, have walking tours that you can take at your own pace by following one of the free maps available from the Convention & Visitors Bureau. The Dayton-Campbell Historic District has 210 structures dating to the last 25 years of the 19th century. German Village, just north of the central business zone and on the river, dates to the early 1800s. Rossville, once a separate city on the west side of the river, was laid out in 1804.

Two historic homes to tour are the Benninghofen House and Butler County Museum, an 1861 Italianate mansion, and the Lane-Hooven House. The first was occupied by the Benninghofen family from 1874 to 1947 and is filled with exquisite antiques, a doll collection, Native American artifacts, a large quilt collection, and a wealth of Civil War memorabilia. It's also the home of the county's historical society and genealogy research records. A rare octagonal house, the 1863 Lane-Hooven mansion has a unique spiral staircase. The public library nearby, which is also octagonal, was the first free library west of the Alleghenies.

Stroll the pretty, downtown Main Street. It's lined with 19th-century buildings, many of them restored as antique shops or trendy restaurants. Note the regal, Second Empire–style courthouse, which was built in 1885, and the Soldiers, Sailors, and Pioneers Monument, which stands on the site of Fort Hamilton. It's open daily except Sunday, is free, and was dedicated on July 4, 1906. A paved, 10-foot-wide, 3.5-mile-long bikeway connects the monument with Joyce Park in south Hamilton. Contrive to come on a summer Saturday, when a colorful farmer's market is set up on Courthouse Square.

From Hamilton, U.S. 27 takes you back to Cincinnati's I-275, which connects you to your choice of north-south and east-west interstates.

For More Information

Greater Cincinnati Convention and Visitors Bureau:
513-621-7862 (local), 800-582-5804 (elsewhere in Ohio), or
800-543-2613 (outside the state)

Oxford Convention and Visitors Bureau: 513-523-8687

Governor Bebb Preserve: 513-867-5835

Alexander House (Oxford): 513-523-1200

Miami University (Oxford): 513-529-2531

Pioneer Farm and House Museum (Oxford): 513-523-6347

Hueston Woods State Park: 513-523-6347 or 800-282-7275
(for lodge reservations only)

Shady-Nook (Millville): 513-863-4343

Greater Hamilton Convention and Visitors Bureau:
800-311-5353

Benninghofen House/Butler County Historical Society and
Museum: 513-896-9930

Lane-Hooven House (Hamilton): 513-863-1389

10

Slip Away in Greene County

Getting there: Greene County adjoins metropolitan Dayton to the east. It is 50 miles from Cincinnati, 200 miles from Cleveland, and 70 miles from Columbus.

Highlights: Dayton's Carillon Park, Xenia's historic area, the Little Miami Scenic Trail, historic Clifton Mill, covered bridges.

Carillon Park in Dayton is a stately landmark set among 65 acres of trees and shrubs. Among its 51 historic buildings are Newcom Tavern, the oldest preserved home in this area; a replica of the Wright Cycle Shop, where the airplane was developed; a section of the Miami and Erie Canal complete with original lock; a 1905 Wright airplane; a 1912 steam locomotive; and much more. To get there, take exit 51 off I-75 and go east on Edwin C. Moses Boulevard, then right on Stewart, and right again on Patterson Boulevard.

For many Ohio families who spend their Sunday afternoons driving country roads, Carillon Park is a first stop on the way out of town because church services are held, year-round, at 7:00 A.M. on Sunday. Favorite hymns are beamed throughout the park from the carillon, and you can hear the entire service in your car.

Carillon Park is open May 1 to October 31, from 10:00 A.M. to 6:00 P.M., Tuesday through Saturday; 1:00 to 6:00 P.M., Sunday; closed on Monday. No admission is charged.

If you're ready for some shopping or dining in an unusual setting, retrace the route to I-75, go north one exit to U.S. 35, and turn east toward Xenia. Make a left on Fairfield Road and follow it for a mile, when you'll spot the Bellfair complex on both sides of the road. It's open every day, except major holidays, until 9:00 P.M.; 8:00 P.M. on Sunday.

Have an old-fashioned soda or a meaty sandwich at the country restaurant, then browse through shops displaying antiques, unusual gifts, arts and crafts, and a year-round Christmas shop. The core of the complex is the Country Stores and Restaurant, centered around a 100-year-old farmhouse. It's decorated, draped, hung, pasted, piled high, and otherwise filled with wacky memorabilia, serious antiques, old advertising signs, iron toys, and dozens of items the whole family will enjoy.

Continue on U.S. 35 into Xenia. Just past the gargoyle-guarded courthouse, which was built in 1901 to replace an earlier building, go three blocks and turn right on Columbus Street, then right again on Second Street, which is one-way to the west. Eden Hall, at 235 East Second Street, has reigned majestically since 1840. This was the home of the fictional Sally Cochran Roush in the movie *And the Ladies of the Club*. Its furnishings and paintings are museum quality, representing a cavalcade of centuries and styles. Mrs. Paul Cozatt will give you a one-hour tour if you arrange it in advance. Admission is charged.

Driving through Xenia, with its stately old streets, you may have the vague feeling that something isn't quite right. Then you notice that the centuries-old trees that canopy old neighborhoods throughout Ohio are missing. Hammers and nails repaired the homes that were damaged in the tornado of 1974, but the oaks and elms will take decades to come back.

If you have time, drive the old streets according to your whim, especially Second Street, then Third Street, which is one-way to the east. They're lined with a treasury of 19th-century mansions. In the heart of it all at 58 South Detroit Street, find Donges Drug Store with its original shelving and a 1899 soda fountain where you can still have phosphates and malts.

Jog left on Church Street and immediately right on North King Street, which brings you to the Greene County Historical Society Complex, comprising an 1876 Queen Anne townhouse, the Carriage House Museum, and the original Galloway Log House, circa 1799, where Tecumseh called on the Galloway family.

Talk was of a romance between the Indian chief and Miss Rebecca, who taught him to read, but in those days, Galloways did not marry Indians. When Tecumseh died in that last bitter battle along the Thames, it is said that Rebecca saw a cloud darken the moon and knew that the Moon Maiden's dark prophecy had come true.

One of the finest biking and hiking trails in the area, the Little Miami Scenic Trail, begins in Xenia. If you want to make a day of biking, park the car and start at the 0.0 Mile Marker near the corner of Church and Detroit. Or, join the 9.6-mile trail (actually part of an 80-mile trail that leads from eastern Cincinnati to Buck Creek State Park near Springfield) at Brush Row Road, where you'll find Mile Marker 3.

This part of the Little Miami Railroad, which ran from Cincinnati to Sandusky, was opened in 1846. The last train came through Xenia in 1966. In 1970, when rail service to Yellow Springs also came to an end, railroading in this area became only another historical has-been.

From Xenia head northeast on U.S. 42. About three miles out, just past Wilberforce University on your right, turn left on Brush Row Road. For a side trip well worth the time, stop at the National Afro-American Museum and Cultural Center. On the original site of Wilberforce University, the center is open Tuesday through Saturday, from 9:00 A.M. to 5:00 P.M.; Sunday, 1:00 to 5:00 P.M.; closed Monday and holidays. Admission is charged.

Leave the museum by continuing west on Brush Row Road for less than a half mile, then turn right on Wilberforce-Clifton Road. In less than a mile, turn left on Jones Road, which leads to a covered bridge, dating to 1873, at Stevenson Road. Retrace your route to Wilberforce Road, turn left, and immediately turn right onto Charleton Mill Road, where you'll see a covered bridge that dates to 1860.

Return to Wilberforce-Clifton Road and turn right for the six-mile drive on a pretty, winding rural road into Clifton, where the six-story Clifton Mill has been grinding since 1802. Today it's the largest operating gristmill in the nation and one of only 47 active mills still remaining. Already an old mill during the Civil War, it worked long hours to grind corn and wheat for the Union army.

Although the Christmas light display here is awesome and worth a special trip, Clifton Mill offers a nostalgic tourist stop any day of the year. In good weather, sit on the deck where you can hear the splashing of the water in the spillway and the creaking of the tireless wheel. In winter, hunker over coffee in the cozy Clifton Mill Restaurant while you wait for a hearty meal of cornmeal mush with sweet syrup, sausage with gravy, or a stick-to-the-ribs soup. Clifton Mill Store and

Mill is open daily, except major holidays, until 3:00 P.M. Hours may vary in winter.

A Side Trip

The area around Xenia was a hotbed of Underground Railroad activity before and during the Civil War. Although most of the homes involved are no longer standing, or are private residences that aren't open to the public, students of African-American history may want to take a drive through the countryside around Xenia to ponder the life-and-death dramas that were played out here during those awful years.

From U.S. 35 head south on U.S. 68 to see the Nosker home at number 550. This was the landing place for runaway slaves, who arrived in cattle cars on the rail line running behind the house. There is evidence that a trap door went to a tunnel and into a cave in the front yard.

Returning north on U.S. 68, cross U.S. 35 and turn right on East Market Street. At 204 was the home of the Reverend Samuel Wilson, a passionate abolitionist. The site is now the Assembly of God church. At number 246, slaves took refuge in a cellar behind the carriage house, which was rumored to have been connected to the main house (circa 1864) by a tunnel.

Turn left on U.S. 42 to see the mansion at number 1120. Now an Omega Psi Phi fraternity house, it was once the home of Colonel Charles Young, the third black American to graduate from West Point. A crack across the road here is directly above a tunnel, said to have been a hiding place for slaves.

Just past this site, turn left on Wilberforce-Clifton Road, where you can only imagine the many lantern-lit farm homes involved in the intrigues. Their names, including the Mitchell House, William Collins Place, and Harding House, were whispered among frightened escapees when they were looking for places to hide. Turn left on Crinnell Road, then left on Clifton Road, where the Ferguson House at 1040 has a trap door leading to a secret, underground room.

Visitors who want to know more about the Underground Railroad in this area will want to visit the National Afro-American Museum and Cultural Center in Wilberforce.

For More Information

Hayton/Montgomery County Convention and Visitors Bureau: 800-221-8234 (Ohio) or 800-221-8235 (U.S.)

Carillon Park (Dayton): 937-293-2841

Bellfair Country Stores and Restaurant: 937-426-0788

Blue Jack (Dayton): 937-376-4318 or 937-427-0879

Eden Hall (Xenia): 937-376-1274

Greene County Historical Society: 937-376-4606

Little Miami Scenic Trail: 937-376-7440

National Afro-American Museum and Cultural Center (Wilberforce): 937-376-4944 or 800-BLK-HIST

Clifton Mill Restaurant: 937-767-5501

Clifton Mill Store and Mill: 937-767-5501

Morgan House Bed and Breakfast (Yellow Springs): 937-767-7509

11

The Secret Side of Warren County

Getting there: Although both Cincinnati and Dayton make good bases for touring Warren County, we've chosen Lebanon and offer four separate day trips. Lebanon is 30 miles north of Cincinnati via I-71 to State 48 and 25 miles south of Dayton on State 48.

Highlights: The Little Miami River; historic Lebanon and the legendary Golden Lamb, Ohio's oldest inn, dating to 1803; Kings Mills (the village, not the theme park); antique shops at Waynesville; Valley Vineyards; pre-Columbian discoveries at Fort Ancient; Fort Ancient State Memorial.

Day One

Any Midwestern tourist over the age of three knows about Paramount's Kings Island, a razzle-dazzle theme park in Warren County, just north of Greater Cincinnati. The park alone should be allotted an entire day or two, especially if you have children. We, however, are off to the country roads of a fast-growing county that still can serve up plenty of pleasant surprises for the shunpiker.

We suggest a day in Lebanon itself and at least two days
for country expeditions, setting your own pace for photogra-
phy, biking or hiking, antiquing, gravestone rubbing, or whatever interests you.

The Golden Lamb, on South Broadway where State 63
and State 48 intersect, has been a haven of hospitality for
almost 200 proud years. Its accommodations are rustic,
antique-filled, and homey—not at all appropriate for the traveler who wants all the new electronic gimmicks. This is a visit
to sweet yesteryear, with all its graces and a few groans.

Breakfast, which is included in the rates and is self-served
in a private dining room upstairs, consists of coffee, sweet
breads, and juices. The Golden Lamb doesn't serve breakfast
to the public, but its fragrant luncheon dishes and its hearty
Ohio dinners attract locals and visitors alike. A favorite day
trip for people from miles around is to come here for lunch
and shopping in the inn's own Lamb Shop.

As you dine, ponder the famous visitors who have stayed
here. They include Charles Dickens, DeWitt Clinton, William
Henry Harrison in 1840, John Quincy Adams in 1845, and
Ulysses S. Grant in 1883. Be sure to read the sign at the
entrance, noting all the notables who have crossed this
threshold.

Even if you're not staying in the inn, don't leave without
touring its corridors upstairs. Rooms that are not occupied
are left open to view. Of special interest is a room filled with
Shaker furniture and artifacts—one of the best collections in
the state. You'll also see Sarah's Room, named for Sarah
Stubbs, who lived here as a child. (Later, you'll travel Stubbs
Mills Road.) The room is decorated with antique children's
furniture and toys as it might have looked when Sarah lived
there.

Parking for guests is plentiful behind the Golden Lamb,
and our walking tours of the city begin there. Just half a block
away is the old Lebanon depot, where you can book a trip on

Golden Lamb, Lebanon

the Turtle Creek Valley Railway. The season runs from April through December, with a large choice of sightseeing and dining excursions as the train tootles its route on the historic tracks between Lebanon and Mason.

The walking tour of Lebanon's East End Historic District was such a pleasure, we took it twice—once to see homes in the morning light and again in the afternoon sun. Here's how:

Start at the Golden Lamb, noting the spacious width of Broadway. Although it was planned a century before automobiles required wider streets, this road was spaced wide enough to allow the turning of a stagecoach and team. Across the street is the regal City Hall, built in 1933.

Walking east on Main Street, you'll immediately pass the oldest building in town at 9 Main Street. It's changed a lot, of course, since it was the home of one of the town's early settlers. At 23 Main, note the shadows of original doors and windows in what was part of National Normal University. A marker commemorating the school is on the grounds of the Golden Lamb.

Continuing up Main, you'll pass a brick Greek Revival home at 116 and an example of Steamboat Gothic at 223. At Main and East Streets, St. Patrick's Episcopal Church was built in 1893 and houses a Spanish convent bell dated 1632.

Turn left on High Street and on the northeast corner is a Second Empire–Style home, circa 1877. Continue right on Mulberry, where you'll see the Orient Fire House, built about 1880. It has changed greatly, but the fire bell, which in past years spelled terror in the town, is still there. Continue east on Mulberry for fine examples of Carpenter Gothic, Queen Anne, and Italianate homes.

Turn left at Silver Street. An early Gothic Revival house dating to 1846 is on one corner, a Queen Anne on another. Heading west on Silver, note the impressive courthouse. Turn right on East Street, then left to Warren Street. The Greek

Revival structure at 215 East Street also was part of the huge National Normal University.

Continuing west on Warren, you'll notice that buildings get older as you return closer to downtown. The First Presbyterian church was built in 1858. Turn left on Cherry Street, where you'll find an African Methodist Episcopal church built by the city's black settlers in 1861. Another church at 116 Cherry, a Gothic Revival, was originally built by German Lutherans.

One of the oldest homes in town, at 115 Silver Street, was built in 1814. At the corner of Silver and Cherry is an "upping block," put there to help people step up into a carriage. Heading east on Silver, you'll pass a Gothic Revival at 213, with its beautiful etched glass. Across from the courthouse is a temple-style Greek Revival house, built circa 1846.

Turn right on East Street, then left on Mulberry. At the corner of Cherry, the miniature "gas station" was built as a taxi stand. Continuing back toward town on Mulberry, you'll pass a Greek Revival masterpiece at 144 and the old lodge hall with its slate mansard roof at 126. Turning left on Broadway takes you back to the Golden Lamb.

After lunch, walk south on Broadway past the classically beautiful library. On your right is the Warren County Historical Society Museum—one of the finest small museums in the Midwest. Schedule at least an hour for the tour of its old shops, household rooms, Shaker rooms, and collections.

For followers of 20th-century history, there is a collection of the works of plastics pioneer Russel Wright (1904–1976), whose original designs include now-collectible Fiesta ware. For qualified researchers, the museum also has an extensive library staffed by knowledgeable volunteers, who know every inch of both the library and the county. Call for hours.

Across Broadway, take a stroll around the depot, where the gift shop is open afternoons except Monday. Then return to the Golden Lamb slowly, lingering at three shops, two of them devoted to antiques and the other—the Golden Turtle Chocolate Factory—to chocolates. Operated by Ohioans Joy and Ted Kossouji, the shop is aswoon with good smells, and the big trays of hand-dipped chocolates are irresistible.

Although the road to Glendower is walkable, it's a steep climb, so we suggest returning to the Golden Lamb for your car. Drive south on Broadway, bearing right just after the depot. In half a mile, turn left at the sign to Glendower.

A masterpiece of Greek Revival architecture, the house was built circa 1836–1840. It's one of a string of such mansions built high on this brow overlooking the town and the river; the others are privately owned. Glendower is furnished in period pieces from more than 400 local pioneer families, giving it an air of lived-in, elegant hominess. It was named by its founder, a young lawyer of Welsh ancestry, for Welsh hero Owen Glendower. The house is open from the first Wednesday in June through the last Sunday in October, weekends only after Labor Day, as well as for special events in December. Hours are Wednesday through Saturday, noon to 4:00 P.M.; Sunday 1:00 to 4:00 P.M. There's a modest admission.

Any time during your stay in Lebanon is a good time to take off on foot, exploring the boutiques and galleries in its immediate downtown area. Marilyn and Ken Haley are typical of the labor-of-love folks who operate businesses here. In the General Store at Good Housekeeping, 9 North Broadway, a retail center since the 1840s, they offer hardware, furniture, gifts, and American antiques. Among their specialties are sleds, wagons, rocking horses, and other children's items.

Good places to eat include the Best Cafe, which is much smarter and more continental than the name implies, and the Village Ice Cream Parlor, offering sandwiches and homemade soups. The only place downtown that is open for Sunday breakfast is the Chili Company at 102 North Broadway. It opens at 6:00 A.M. daily.

Day Two

Leave Lebanon by driving northeast on U.S. 42, the Cincinnati-Columbus Road. You'll see magnificent farm homes dating to the early 19th century, their fields still green with corn and their barnyards filled with fat, busily pecking hens.

Turn left on State 73, then immediately right on Main Street. Another village that was founded well before Ohio became a state, Waynesville was surveyed about 1792 and settled in 1797 by a group of Englishmen who planned to turn it into a plantation. They bought more than 10 tons of supplies at Baltimore, hauled them to Philadelphia, and floated them down the Allegheny and Monongahela to the Ohio. Eventually they reached this spot on the Little Miami River, built log cabins, and platted a town much like an English village.

It was here that the first steam engine was invented in 1801 (the inventors were never able to get a patent or backing) and the first commercially grown chewing tobacco in the United States was planted. The Stetson hat was invented here. So was branch banking and one of the most famous horse liniments of its time, Dr. Robb's Hippodrome Liniment. A host of harebrained schemes were pawned here as well, including pearl farming, pecan growing, gas wells, a cracker bakery, rice fields, and cotton crops. All of them flopped.

Despite itself, Waynesville prospered. It not only was on the Little Miami River, a major artery, but also was near the Bullskin Trace, a trail that was cut in 1773 to link the Ohio River basin with Detroit and the Great Lakes. Daniel Boone, once captured by the Shawnee, is said to have escaped via the Bullskin Trace.

By 1844 Waynesville had a rail line. It had been a stagecoach stop far longer, evidenced by the establishment in 1822 of the Hammel House Inn.

Because it also was handy to the Miami Canal, on which Waynesville farmers could send their produce to hungry

Cincinnati, growers grew richer. Finding a ready market for their sauerkraut, they shipped it by the hundreds of barrels. The city has for years honored its famous kraut by holding the Ohio Sauerkraut Festival the second weekend of each October. Try the sauerkraut in every form, including brownies.

One of Waynesville's flesh-and-blood attractions is historian Dennis E. Dalton, who gives guided tours to groups and has established a new tearoom, the Angel in the Garden. Stop by for a bit of history, or ask Dennis for a ghost story. He'll tell you that Waynesville is Ohio's most haunted town. He's available at very modest rates to ride along in your car and point out the sights. To make arrangements, call 513-897-8855.

Also of historical importance is the Quaker meetinghouse, the oldest west of the Alleghenies. The large and active Quaker community here was founded by Dr. John Evans, who was appointed territorial governor of Colorado in 1862 by President Lincoln, and who founded Northwestern University.

Park at the first opportunity and strike out on foot. Street parking is usually available except during special events when shuttle buses (often hayrides) run between parking areas and downtown. In such cases, follow the signs to parking.

On both sides of the street in the six blocks between State 73 and Franklin Street, you'll find more than 35 antique shops plus art galleries, specialty shops, snacks, and dining. The Chamber of Commerce, a good place to stop for information, is located in the middle of the route on Main between High and Miami.

The Hammel House Inn at 121 South Main Street has hosted thousands of wayfarers over the century, among them John D. Rockefeller and J. P. Morgan. A simple, homespun inn with its original brick walls bared, it was built as a stagecoach stop in 1822. Today it serves lunch only and reservations are recommended, especially on weekends.

The Hammel House also has an extensive gift shop selling crafts, quilts, antiques, and Ohioana. Lodgings upstairs have private baths and include breakfast. "No pets, no smoking, no television, no children under ten," promise the proprietors.

Head west out of town on Franklin Road, which is Old Route 73, or on State 73, which brought you into town. They merge. Look to your right, high on a hill, where there is a mansion. In the 1840s, it was the home of the world-famous Haines Sanitarium. You may have seen the Haines home in town on Third Street, just a stone's throw from the Episcopal church, which was attended by Tennessee Williams when he came to Waynesville to visit his grandparents.

Nobody knows today exactly what was in Dr. James Haines's "Golden Specific," or how it worked in curing alcoholism, but what *is* known is that it contained extract of catalpa and was served in tea. Its fame spread all over the United States as cured alcoholics gave their testimonials, and the cure appears to have been genuine. By 1890, Haines's reputation had reached London and he opened an office there. No record can be found of the project after World War I.

Retracing your route the short distance back through Waynesville on State 73, cross the Little Miami River and turn left on Smith Road. You'll arrive in Corwin, which is yet another of Ohio's picturebook, historic settlements. It's also a hub of activity for the Little Miami Scenic Trail. Bicycles can be rented here, and you can also get homemade-style ice cream.

Return to State 73 and head east through beautiful lake and park scenery to Harveysburg—one of Ohio's oldest black communities and an important stop on the Underground Railroad. Its older streets are a ghost town of interesting old homes; its beautiful high school, built in 1936, is abandoned. Neat, new neighborhoods are quickly replacing the old parts of the village, and it's hoped that the black school museum, at Wall Street and Old Route 73, will survive.

The museum is housed in one of the area's earliest schools

for blacks, the Elizabeth Harvey Free School, which was built in 1829 and in 1831 became the first school for black children in the Northwest Territory.

Retrace your route west on State 73 because this is the simplest way and also a beautiful drive back across the Caesar Creek Reservoir. Two miles past the bridge, watch for an acute left turn on Clarksville Road, also County 37. In two miles, this takes you to the scenic overlook above Caesar Creek Reservoir. At the state park's visitors center, browse among the displays showing the natural history of the area.

The name is thought to have come from an escaped slave named Cizar. Passing through the area on a flatboat, he was captured in 1776 by the Shawnee, who adopted him. He enjoyed fishing a particular creek and named it for himself. When Ohio folk hero Simon Kenton planned his own escape from the Shawnee, Cizar advised him to follow Caesar Creek to the Little Miami, shunning the Indian trail along the west bank.

The valley, which winds its way south to Fort Ancient State Memorial, has been inhabited for at least 11,000 years. Adena and Hopewell peoples lived here starting about 1000 B.C., followed by the Fort Ancient culture, whose earthworks have been found throughout the area. They are known to have traded far and wide. Copper came from Lake Superior; shark and animal teeth found here show that they traded with ocean peoples. Obsidian from the Rocky Mountains and mica from the Carolinas have also been found. Archaeological studies go on in the area, although many of the mounds and serpentine walls have been destroyed by waves of settlers and developers.

Early settlers speculated that the earthen walls were fortifications to ward off mastadon attacks, or were used as a corral to round up bison for butchering. In the 1930s, studies concluded that the ditches and walls had some ceremonial use, perhaps related to the solar system. New findings at Fort

Ancient State Memorial continue to unravel Ohio's rich and captivating Indian history.

Pick up brochures and maps at the Caesar Creek State Park Visitor Center and plan your time according to your interests. The park has fishing, hunting, picnicking, hiking, horse trails, swimming, boating, and much more. For those with a family, it may be worth an entire day or even several.

As you leave Caesar Creek State Park Visitor Center, continue south on Clarksville Road for a mile and a half and turn left on County 12, Oregonia Road. About a mile after crossing Flat Fork, turn left on Township 292 into the Pioneer Village— another of the many log-cabin villages that dot Ohio. This is an entire community built around a clean and spacious village green. The log cabins are authentic, dating to as early as 1795, although they were moved here from original sites throughout the area.

The village is especially lively during special events, which start with the maple syrup camp in March and go through Halloween at the Village in late October. Hours and events vary, so call ahead.

Leaving the village, turn right on Oregonia Road, County 12. After about three miles, when you reach the dead end at Corwin Road, turn right for two miles and, just past Elbon Road, you'll see a covered bridge and the entrance to Caesar Creek Gorge State Nature Preserve.

The hiking trail here follows the breathtaking gorge, then wends through the thickly wooded beech, maple, hickory, and oak forest. Watch for wild orchid, shooting stars, and other wildflowers. You may also find unique fossils, which were left as glacial melt wore through the limestone and shale.

Retrace your route south on Corwin Road to Oregonia, where you can turn right to cross the Little Miami. Following

Oregonia Road's zigzag route takes you the six miles back to Lebanon through farm country that is developing but still has many century-old farmhouses. If you get lost as the road wanders, keep heading east and you'll butt into Lebanon.

An alternate route, if you have time to spare, is to continue south on Corwin Road, Township 47, out of Oregonia to Mathers Mills. Turn left on Wilmington Road, cross I-71, and continue south (right) on Middleboro Road for two miles, then go right on State 350. Signs lead you to Fort Ancient where there are Indian mounds and a see-forever view of the river valley that was so sacred to early tribes. The museum tells the story of the Fort Ancient peoples and takes the visitor through centuries of Indian history.

State 350 takes you west and joins State 123, which will return you to Lebanon. Another short detour is to Irons Fruit Farm. Two miles after State 123 crosses I-71, look for Stubbs Mills Road on your left. About a mile later, on your left, turn into the farm.

In addition to a nine-month display of seasonal produce (they are closed in the winter), Irons Fruit Farm also lets you pick your own strawberries, tart cherries, red raspberries, blackberries, and blueberries, while in season. Jams, apple butters, cider, and baked goods are for sale as well. Half a dozen apple varieties, plus pumpkins, sweet corn, squash, and all the other country favorites are here in abundance. Best of all, the Irons family loves animals and hopes you do too. Visit their petting zoo to schmooze with the friendly burros, pigs, and deer.

Day Three

Leave Lebanon westbound on State 63 for about four miles and turn right on State 741. Within half a mile, at Otterbein, a mammoth Victorian mansion rises incongruously out of the rapidly urbanizing farmland. Today it's a senior-citizen center but it once was the heart of a powerful Shaker farming commune. The complex was doomed because Shaker practice prohibited sex. No new members were born into the faith, which grew only as converts were made—an uphill battle because the faithful had to sign away everything they owned, as well as their love lives.

In time, conversions waned and older Shakers died. Unable to sustain itself, the community sold its lands and died out early in the 20th century.

As you continue north, State 741 follows the bed of Shaker Creek through rapidly changing landscapes—a meadow here, a cornfield there, pockets of new homes, fallow fields, fallen barns. Subdivisions seem to be taking over, but we still found this a route worthy of the "country roads" theme.

When State 741 intersects State 122 and State 123 in about four miles, you'll find yourself in Red Lion. At this intersection, note the classic country church, which was built in 1853, and Mom's Restaurant, where state patrolmen stop for biscuits and gravy in the morning or slabs of Mom's homemade pie for snacks. Stop in if it's open.

Continue north on State 741 for three miles toward Springboro. Just past Ryan Road on your right, turn right onto Red Lion–Five Points Road, and in less than a mile watch for the old Null family cemetery on your right. The Nulls were among the original settlers, 1796–1816, and the stories on their gravestones tell volumes. In the distance, rustic Hawkscrest Farm is an American still life, framed in fencing and timeless as the soil.

Turn left onto Lower Springboro Road and stop at Kesling Park on your right to stretch your legs, if you like. Another mile west on Lower Springboro Road brings you out on State 741 again, in the heart of Springboro's historic district.

As we suggested in Waynesville, it's best to park your car at the first opportunity and strike off on foot, up one side of

Main Street and down the other. The scene seems frozen in time; its historic buildings were preserved and cherished as they were converted into a charming shopping village.

Sally's Quilts at 250 South Main was the home of the family of famed artist Grant Wood; it dates to 1832.

The Brass Pig Tea Room at 245 South Main is named for the porkers that brought such wealth to this area. The building was built as a general store by town founder Jonathon Wright about 1835. The restaurant serves Monday through Saturday from 11:00 A.M. to 3:00 P.M.; closed Sunday. Reservations are suggested. The home of Jonathon Wright can be seen at 80 State Street. Privately owned, it has a dual stairway and cherry woodwork.

Prim Roses is a boutique housed in a regal Victorian mansion.

A tiny building on Main Street now known as the Olde Village Framing and Crosstitching shop was originally the springhouse for the large home nearby. It was once the home of Nathan Hunt, who became secretary to the great scientist Booker T. Washington.

At 245 South Main, look at the local Grange Hall. A secret society that sprang up in the 1870s and was originally called the Patrons of Husbandry, granges grew in popularity and peppered this part of Ohio. You'll see their timeworn meeting halls throughout the country roads of the state.

If you want to make an evening of it, the Miami Valley Dinner Theatre in Springboro is a good-time favorite. Call for reservations and to see what's playing.

When you're ready to leave Springboro, head west on State 73, which is also West Central Avenue, to number 155. This house, which is on the National Register of Historic Homes, and the other white mansion across the street are not open to the public, so enjoy them from the road. They were built in 1887 for Jonathon Wright's son and grandson. Well into the 1990s, the beautiful old home was occupied until her death by Anna Null Doyle, who had come here as a child in 1906. Built in 1857, it still had most of its original furnishings including the bed that had arrived on a wagon with Mrs. Doyle's grandparents.

The most direct route back to your lodgings in Lebanon is to head south on State 741, then at Red Lion take State 123 south into Lebanon.

For a daylight return, head east on State 73 back through Springboro toward Waynesville. After about three miles, turn south on State 48. The corner at the intersection, site of an early Quaker meetinghouse, is now a touristy, but fun-looking, shopping strip. Windmill Farm Market spills over with fresh fruits and vegetables, including pick-your-own crops in season. Also sold here are baked goods, herbs, nursery stock, plants, and flowers.

Farther south on State 48, on your left at number 5474, watch for the Hidden Valley Fruit Farm and the covered bridge nearby. Browse the marketplace in a 150-year-old barn for the foods that have been standards for the 200 years that these fields have been farmed. Amish butter and cheese are for sale, plus baked goods, fresh produce, antiques, and pottery. The farm is open Monday through Saturday from 9:00 A.M. to 8:00 P.M., Sunday from 11:00 A.M. to 6:00 P.M. in spring.

The road back to Lebanon takes you through more mill country. In the years when water power provided most of the energy here, the Springboro area had dozens of mills: gristmills, sawmills, feed mills, and at least one woolen mill. Today, only the river remains.

Day Four

Don't start too early in the day because our goal is to end up with one of the famous steak cookout evenings at Valley Vineyards. Although we haven't made it a part of our country roads tour, Paramount's Kings Island theme park is also in the area. It should be an excursion for a separate day.

To make this southern swing out of Lebanon, head south on State 48, which takes you once again across the sparkling Little Miami River and its 50-mile riverside trail.

Just over a mile past the bridge, make a right turn on Grandin Road, which is also County 150. Suddenly you're in another world as the road sweeps steeply down to the river at a place that had been known as The Gorge. Out of nowhere appears the ghost of a giant industrial complex. And therein lies a tale.

The Peters Cartridge Company, with its sky-high shot tower (molten lead was dropped down the tower to form pellets), is only part of what was once a pulsing industrial power center. It all began along these riverbanks in about 1880, when a dam and millrace were built here by Joseph King, who had already made his mark in the world of ammunition at the Miami Powder Company in Xenia. For three miles, small structures were built along the river, all of them used in the production of black powder. One of the key ingredients, charcoal, was abundant here, made from the black willow trees that blanketed the hillsides.

The purpose of so many buildings was to keep them isolated so volatile ingredients couldn't mix accidentally, and to minimize damage from the explosions that began to rattle the valley with thrilling regularity. In a further safety move, horses that pulled the powder wagons were shod with brass shoes and copper nails. Examples of these are in the Kings Mills display at the Warren County Historical Society Museum in Lebanon, described in Day One.

In time, precautions became even more strict. Networks of plumbing threaded the area with frequent fireplugs and automatic sprinklers in each building. Although tons of munitions were shipped, most explosions were minor. The worst occurred in 1890, when a number of laborers and some children who lived nearby were killed. The King operation became two operations when Peters Cartridge was added.

By 1878, the mills employed a thousand men, women, and children, and had their own water and power works. The river and the railroad that ran along it rang with commercial traffic. It is hard to envision this today, where silence is broken only by the sibilant song of the river.

When Peters introduced the first machine-loaded shotgun shells, sales soared, aided by Annie Oakley and Buffalo Bill, who were hired as spokespersons. Although the disastrous flood of 1913 took out the bridge and did extensive damage to the mills, business bounded back bigger than ever.

Workers thronged in from Cincinnati on a trolley line that ran here until the 1920s. In 1934, Peters Cartridge Company was sold to Remington, and during World War II, 5,000 people were employed by the bulging munitions works. Young ladies could earn as much as $12 a week, and they flocked here for jobs.

In 1950, the remaining plant was sold to Seagram's and used as a storehouse for whiskey. The huge fields beyond the factory, once a shooting range, are now the site of Paramount's Kings Island theme park.

By the 1970s, the grounds were deserted and vandalized. We can't guess what will be there when you arrive, but during our visit, most of the windows were broken and debris was everywhere. However, repairs were in progress and a company was offering office space for lease. Even in its derelict state, the works are awesome in size and humming with long-forgotten stories.

Regardless of the factories' fate, there will always be much to see along the river, which has been preserved as a scenic parkway for horse, bicycle, and foot traffic. If you don't have time for a hero hike along the entire 50-mile trail, start here and ramble for as long as you like through shady hillsides covered with mulberry and blackberry and hidden fortunes in old foundations and machinery, before returning to your car.

Continue west on Grandin Road across the river, up the steep hill to the community of Kings Mills. A typical mill town, it has a church, school, library, and store—all built by the mill. At the end of King Street, the original King mansion is still occupied by a King family member. Many of the original row houses, which in their heyday rented for $7 per month, remain.

Still, the town is a shadow of what it was in the days when it had three hotels including one with 250 rooms, a movie theater, and everything except "saloons to disturb the peace," according to an old advertisement.

Kings Mills Road continues west as it turns from country to busy suburbs. Watch for a left turn on Columbia Road, just before I-71. Just past the junior high school, which you'll see on your left, look to your right at the corner of Wilson Road for the Kings Mills General Store and Christmas Shop. One of this neighborhood's few remaining old buildings, it has been turned into a Christmas fairyland.

Ron and Mary Claire Greene have collected Christmas wonders from all over the world. These objects are displayed on shelves, hanging from the ceiling, and on half a dozen fully decorated, themed Christmas trees, which take your breath away even in July. The shop is filled with twinkling lights, good smells, gifts, collectibles, and items for the current holiday in addition to the year-round Christmas collection. Open daily from Easter through Christmas, Kings Mills General Store extends its hours to 9:00 P.M. during busy seasons. Call ahead for specifics.

Return to Kings Mills Road, which becomes State 741 as it crosses I-71, and go west a mile. When State 741 makes a sharp right, turn left on the continuation of Kings Mills

Road, passing through a mile of subdivision. Go left on U.S. 42, which becomes Mason's Main Street.

Continuing into town on Main Street, park in the Yost Pharmacy lot, which is handy to most of the stops you'll want to make including the Chamber of Commerce at 316 West Main Street, where you can pick up the latest information.

The PTD & CO., a gift shop, now housed in the old brick Mason Hotel at 101 East Main Street, displays its ware in 10 rooms that have changed little since the day in 1901 when Rebecca McClung was murdered here. The hotel dates to 1878 and is a treasury of wreaths, potpourris, children's items, antiques, and accessories for the home.

From Yost Pharmacy go west to the corner of Main and North East Street. Turn right onto North East, go north one block, and turn left on Church Street. The third house on the left, at 207 Church Street, is the Alverta Green Museum. Built in 1900, the house became the home of Alverta Green in 1942. When she died in 1988, she willed her home to the Mason Historical Society. The house preserves the flavor of small town America at the turn of the century. Exhibits in each room highlight various aspects of Mason's history. The Alverta Green Museum is open from 1:00 to 4:00 P.M. on Thursday and Friday and on other days by appointment. Call the curator, Lucy Gorsuch, at 513-398-6750 for more information.

Ye Olde Wash House Gift Shoppe, behind the museum, is located in what was once the home's wash house. Here you will find antiques, old photographs of Mason, and button jewelry. The shop keeps the same hours as the museum.

When you're finished with your explorations in Mason, hop back on U.S. 42 northbound. (Incidentally, the restaurant at the Houston Motel, north of Mason at 4026 U.S. 42, is locally famous for its enormous salad bar, prime rib, and frog's legs.) Just past the intersection of State 741, turn right on Mason-Morrow Road (County 38). Stay with it east through South Lebanon, following the "truck route" signs. Continue east, following the same road, also called Road 38, which follows the river in all its glory.

Two miles past South Lebanon, just after crossing Baker Creek, turn left on Stubbs Mills Road (County 35) and after another mile and a half, turn right on Shawhan Road. In less than two miles, you're at the original David T. Smith Workshops and Showroom.

Smith has his own forge, pottery, wood shop, and a crew of workers to turn out the reproduction antiques that have made him nationally famous. In addition to his signature furniture line, he also reproduces redware—the pottery that was so much a part of early Warren County history. Roam the rustic grounds, watch artisans at work, and shop for gifts or custom-made furniture. The complex is open year-round, Tuesday through Saturday, from 10:00 A.M. to 5:00 P.M.

Continue east on Shawhan until it dead-ends at Waynesville Road, then turn right for half a mile, left for half a mile, and at State 123, turn right into Morrow.

A quaint, old river town, Morrow makes a very good base for canoeing the Little Miami or bicycling the Little Miami Scenic Trail. Rentals are available. The town offers some interesting shops if you want to nose around a bit. On Pike Street, west of the bridge, are the Creative Arts Studio and Morrow Antiques, located in a historic church.

Now we're off to Valley Vineyards, which has been showered with national and international awards for its Ohio wines. From Morrow, turn right off State 123 to the joint routes of U.S. 22 and State 3 for two and a half miles.

For three generations, the Schuchters have carried on the family tradition of winemaking, today producing more than a dozen varieties of wine from their own and other local grapes. These include Blue Eye, a dry red made from an American hybrid grape; Hillside Red, made from a blend of French hybrid grapes; and their distinctive white Seyval. There's also a Chablis, a blush, sweet Concords and Catawbas, and a Niagara from America's oldest white grape. Among house specialties is mead, a honey wine that is rarely found, even in boutique wineries like this one.

Hours for the showroom and wine tastings are 11:00 A.M. to 8:00 P.M. on Monday through Thursday, 11:00 A.M. to 11:00 P.M. on Friday and Saturday, and 1:00 to 6:00 P.M. on Sunday. A wine festival, held the last weekend in September, draws thousands of oenophiles, many of them in their RVs, from throughout the East.

If you're lucky enough to be in Morrow on a Friday or Saturday night, make reservations for Valley Vineyards' famous steak cookout.

Route 22/23 west leads you past Isaacs' Shaker Hill, built in 1863 and now a shop specializing in handcrafted furniture and Santas, pottery, tinware, quilts, and carvings. Continue west on 22/23 through rolling farmlands. If you brake for antique shops, the route gives you several to choose from at Zoar and Hopkinsville. Here, at State 48, turn right and drive the eight miles into Lebanon, or in three miles, you're at exit 28 on I-71.

A Side Trip: The Little Miami River

The Little Miami River starts north of Yellow Springs, which lies outside Warren County, and gathers beauty and strength as it makes its way—sometimes whispering, sometimes rampaging—to the Ohio River. Great volumes of Ohio history have traveled on it, and the river is as important a recreation resource today as it was a commercial tool yesterday.

Nowhere is its spell felt more magically than in Warren County. The entire length of the Little Miami through the county is accompanied by a 50-mile strip of abandoned railroad right-of-way that is now part of a 60-mile trail from Yellow Springs south to Milford in Clermont County. It's used by bicyclists, roller bladers, hikers, horseback riders, and picnickers along its entire length. If you prefer to drive with the best view of the river along the way, the best bets are Corwin Road from Wilmington Road north into Corwin and Mason-Morrow-Millgrove Road from South Lebanon to Morrow.

Shawnee chief Tecumseh was born in this valley. Daniel Boone knew well its secrets, both as an explorer and as a prisoner of the Shawnee. Eons before modern tribes arrived, the ancient Mound Builders built miles of unexplained mounds and earthworks on its banks. And eons before that, nature's sculptors scraped the valley deep between soaring cliffs in some areas and widened it in others to create muck lands rich with nutrients.

Our routes cross and recross the Little Miami many times, visiting its villages and making pilgrimages to its parks. Although U.S. 42 roughly follows the river through this area, there is no one, unbroken road that can be driven to follow its banks.

If, however, you want to walk all or parts of the trails in Little Miami Scenic State Park or put your canoe into the river itself, contact the Warren County Convention and Visitors Bureau.

Although this book is about country roads, the Jeremiah Morrow Bridge, which crosses the river on the interstate (I-71) near Fort Ancient, is worth a look because it's the second-longest span in the state. The view of the Little Miami river gorge from the scenic overlook at the bridge is spectacular.

The overlook-park complex, which is divided into three sections that are connected by scenic driveways, offers roadside rest facilities with an excellent tourist information office, picnic tables, grills, and nature trails. We hopped onto the interstate for just this one stretch, solely to enjoy the view, the park, and the facilities.

About the Quakers and Shakers

Because Ohio travelers encounter so many sites connected with one or the other of these religions, it's important to know the difference. Today, the Quaker faith survives and is as mainstream a modern religion as any other. The Shakers, whose only growth came from conversions because the sexes were not permitted to mingle, died out.

Both groups had important roles in bringing schools and culture to Ohio. Both were active in the abolitionist movement and in helping runaway slaves escape via the Underground Railroad to northern states and to Canada.

The first Quaker meetinghouse west of the Alleghenies was built at Waynesville. It survives today as a place of worship. The first Shakers who settled in Ohio came to the Lebanon area and, by 1810, had a thriving settlement of 300 members. They farmed the rich bottomlands along the Little Miami, living a communal existence.

On entering the Shaker community, converts signed over all their belongings to the United Society of Believers in Christ's Second Appearing. Because they usually achieved their zeal after a heavenly "visitation" that left them shaking, they became known as Shakers.

Superb breeders, except when it came to their own kind, Shakers developed hardy new strains of corn and tomatoes, and sold their seeds in bright packages. Their handmade brooms were a source of income for their community at Union Village (1805–1913). The Shakers also developed the Poland China pig, which became so important a factor in Ohio's economy that a monument to it was built outside of the village of Blue Ball. At the height of the madness that resulted from this passion for pork, Poland China boars sold for as much as $60,000 early in the 20th century.

Well before that, the Shakers had almost died out. So husbandry of their China pig strain, which also had become known as the Warren County pig, was taken over by a Pole named Asher Asher. Hence, it became the Poland China.

In addition to the many Shaker artifacts found in museums throughout the state, their chief remaining monument is the Otterbein Home on State 741, just north of State 63 west of Lebanon. Now a senior citizens center, it is an impressive complex including an enormous Victorian building and a number of stalwart outbuildings.

For More Information

Warren County Convention and Visitors Bureau:
   800-791-4FUN, Website: www.Ohio4fun.org

The Golden Lamb: 513-932-5065

Turtle Creek Valley Railway and gift shop (Lebanon):
   513-398-8584

Warren County Historical Society Museum: 513-932-1817

General Store at Good Housekeeping (Lebanon):
   513-932-1881

Best Cafe (Lebanon): 513-932-4400

Village Ice Cream Parlor and Restaurant (Lebanon):
   513-932-6918

Chili Company (Lebanon): 513-932-8855

Hammel House Inn (Waynesville): 513-897-2333 or
   513-897-3779

Caesar Creek State Park Visitor Center: 513-897-1050

Caesar Creek Pioneer Village: 513-897-1120

Irons Fruit Farm: 513-932-2853

Mom's Restaurant (Red Lion): 513-746-0150

Sally's Quilts and Gifts (Springboro): 513-748-1992

The Brass Pig Tea Room (Springboro): 513-748-2546

Prim Roses (Springboro): 513-748-3009

Olde Village Framing and Crosstitching (Springboro):
513-748-9555

Miami Valley Dinner Theatre (Springboro): 513-746-4554 or
800-677-9505

Windmill Farm Market (State 73 between Waynesville and
Springboro): 937-885-3965

Hidden Valley Fruit Farm (north of Lebanon): 513-932-1869

Kings Mills General Store and Christmas Shop: 513-398-1677
or 800-327-5639

Mason Chamber of Commerce: 513-398-2188

PTD & CO. (Mason): 513-398-1558

Houston Motel Restaurant (Mason): 513-398-7377

David T. Smith Workshops and Showroom (Morrow):
513-932-2472

Morrow Antiques (Morrow): 513-899-3366

Valley Vineyards (Morrow): 513-899-2485

Isaacs' Shaker Hill (Morrow): 513-899-2927

12

Merrily on to Marietta

Getting there: Found where I-77 crosses the Ohio River, Marietta is 190 miles from Cincinnati, 170 miles from Cleveland, and 120 miles from Columbus.

Highlights: Historic Marietta and the country roads of Washington County.

Just as the Golden Lamb is a must-see in Lebanon, Marietta's premier hotel, the Lafayette, is the place to call home while touring Washington County. It's a full-service hotel situated at the riverfront where the Muskingum meets the Ohio. Overlooking the monument where early settlers scrambled up the riverbanks into unbroken wilderness, the hotel has a view of sunsets on the Ohio River and is within walking distance of most of the historic points of interest.

Even if you're not lodging here, don't miss a tour of the Lafayette. Near the elevators, note the high-water mark from the 1937 flood, which deposited 10.5 feet of water in the lobby. Outside the building, another marker shows the level reached by the 1913 flood.

Built in 1918, the Lafayette is named for the French hero who had visited this very spot in 1825. Today the hotel has spacious rooms and all the modern conveniences, but its corridors hum with history. Browse around to see the gift shop, the original call-bell system salvaged from the old Mansion House, an 11-foot pilot wheel suspended from the lobby ceiling, and the impressive long-rifle collections. The guns were handcrafted between 1760 and 1890.

An entire day can be spent in a walking or driving tour of Marietta's streets and lanes. Right outside the hotel is the cobblestoned waterfront with its pretty gazebo and historic markers explaining the landing of the first settlers. Proceeding up Front Street, you'll pass the *Becky Thatcher* showboat, an authentic sternwheeler built in 1928, now featuring a restaurant and lounge on the upper deck and a theater on the lower deck where spectators can "hiss" and "boo" at the villains in melodramas.

As you continue up Front Street, you'll see superb examples of Greek Revival architecture, a Congregational church built in 1906 for a congregation that organized in 1796, and Muskingum Park with its handsome pavilion and a memorial sculpted by Gutzon Borglum, the sculptor of Mount Rushmore. The stately home on the corner of Scammel Street was built in 1806 for the fourth governor of Ohio, Return Jonathan Meigs, who later became a U.S. senator, then postmaster general.

A marker on the street commemorates the arrival of the first families (whose names are listed) on August 19, 1788. The Ohio River Museum complex on the riverfront near here includes a 1918 steamboat—the sole survivor of what was once an enormous fleet of steam towboats. The museum is open March through November.

One street over, at Second and Washington, the Campus Martius Museum is on the site of the original stockade of the same name. Both the Ohio River and Campus Martius Museums are operated by the Ohio Historical Society and are open the same hours, which vary seasonally. Call ahead. Admission is charged. Enclosed by the museum and on its original site is the home of General Rufus Putnam, who led

Ohio River Museum, Marietta

the first settlers. Also on the site is the original Ohio Company Land Office, the oldest surviving building in the Northwest Territory.

Turn right on Sacra Via. The name, meaning Sacred Way in Latin, was used by the original pioneers when they found a graded thoroughfare that the prehistoric Mound Builders had laid from the river to their elevated gathering place. Continue to Fifth Street and turn right onto a street of mansions and the traditional Carnegie Library, which has always been so much a part of Ohio village life.

Note the Mound Cemetery on your left. Originally the burial mound of a Hopewell chief, it was adopted as a cemetery by white settlers in 1788. Buried here are many of the original settlers and, it is believed, more Revolutionary War officers than in any other cemetery. There is a good reason. At the end of the war, officers were paid in scrip that could be exchanged for land in the Northwest Territory (which would not become the State of Ohio until 1803). In order to claim their land, they had to come in person. They settled here, died here, and were buried here.

Of special interest at 331 Fifth Street is the House of Seven Porches, which is featured on the Trolley Tour and on the historic walking tour map of the city. (It's no longer a bed-and-breakfast.) Note the house next to it at 322 Fifth Street. It's baronial by today's building standards, yet it arrived in pieces that were labeled and numbered—one of the many Sears Roebuck kit houses that were built throughout the Midwest early in this century.

Turning right on Putnam Street, you'll see the Betsey Mills Club on your right. Built as a club for women and girls in the days when women were expected to "keep their place," it's still a social center. Its popular Early American dining room is open to the public of both sexes. Across the street is the campus of Marietta College, chartered in 1835. The magnificent Greek Revival president's home was built in 1818; Erwin Hall, with its landmark clock tower, was built in 1850.

Take a peek inside the City Hall on your right, which you're welcome to do, then turn right on Third Street and stop in at the Marietta Convention and Visitors Bureau, located on the first floor of a stunning home built in 1868. The architect was later commissioned to oversee the restoration of France's Versailles Palace. In addition to offering brochures and information, the folks there are glad to let you look around at the home's beautiful original features.

If you have time, ramble farther up and down Second, Third, and Fourth Streets, passing entire neighborhoods of mansions, one after another. Except for modern cars in the street, the scene could be the turn of the century, perfectly sealed in time. The Castle, a historic house museum at 418 Fourth Street, is one of the best examples of Gothic Revival architecture in Ohio, complete with its own carriage house. Many of the furnishings and displays are original to the house; the rest of the furnishings are from other Marietta homes. A video tells the story of the house and families who lived here. Note Larchmont, a southern colonial mansion at 524 Second Street. Built in 1824, it's featured on the historic walking tour map and on the Trolley Tour.

Is it lunchtime yet? Return to the Lafayette, or try the Levee House Cafe, the only remaining Ohio River riverfront building. Included on its menu are Rossi's pastas, which are made in Marietta and are sold in gourmet shops all over the nation. (The factory is near the hotel; stop in for a free catalog listing Rossi's own sauces, as well as such gourmet pastas as saffron, calamari, tomato basil garlic, artichoke, and many more.) Dinner at the Levee is also recommended.

The other half of a Marietta tour is Historic Harmar Village on the other side of the river. Drive across the Washington Street Bridge and turn right on Lancaster Street, then left on Bartlett. It's a steep and narrow climb, not recommended for RV campers. This is Lookout Point, where you'll have a bird's-eye view of the river and the surrounding area.

Heading toward the river down Maple Street, turn right on Fort Harmar Drive, then left on Market Street. Here, in a tiny pocket of land carved by the two rivers, is the site of the original Fort Harmar, built in 1785, and the Henry Fearing House, dating to the 1840s, which was destined for demolition until it was rescued by the county historical society.

Tours are available Saturday and Sunday afternoons, April 1 through October 31 for a modest donation. Historic Harmar Village is one of the city's best places to browse, shop, and stroll. There's a model railroad museum, a pub, and lots of little nooks and crannies.

The stone Putnam home, dating to 1805, was Marietta's first bank. In this tiny area you'll also find the Children's Toy and Doll Museum, Attic Treasures antiques, a Coca-Cola Museum, and the Harmar Tavern, open Monday through Saturday for breakfast and lunch and Sunday 9:00 A.M. to 11:00 P.M. Also on Maple Street is Harper's Landing, where local crafters offer their wares daily, except Sunday.

Although our directions brought you to West Marietta by car so you could drive up to Lookout Point, Historic Harmar Village is also a pleasant walk via a pedestrian bridge, once a railroad bridge in heavy use from 1873 to 1962.

At one time, Washington County had more than 50 covered bridges. Ten of them, located on the county's most scenic and remote country roads, remain. Our route loops west out of Marietta, then east out of Marietta, forming a figure 8. Some of the roads are gravel but were in excellent condition during our visit. If you're here at a time when flooding is severe, check ahead with the highway patrol before venturing into *terra incognita.*

Leaving Marietta across the Washington Street Bridge, turn right onto State 676 into Churchtown, then Watertown. You'll pass two classic, old-world churches, St. John the Baptist Catholic Church, built in 1866, and a German Lutheran Church, which is almost as old.

If you're a golfer and have your clubs along, you may want to spend part of your day rounding the nines at the Lakeside Golf Course (on State 60) in Beverly, which overlooks the Muskingum. If so, turn north off State 676 in Watertown, picking up State 339 to Beverly.

Otherwise, at the far side of Watertown, turn right on State 339 and in just over two miles turn left on Township 172. In half a mile, you'll see the Harra Covered Bridge, built about 1870 over the south branch of Wolf Creek.

Return to State 339, turn right, and go five miles to Township 29, then bear right as the road joins Township 39. It's about a mile and a half to the Bell Covered Bridge, built in 1888.

Stay on Township 39, which takes you past an old family cemetery and back to State 676. Turn left, go just over a mile, then turn left on State 6. Turn right at the first opportunity, County 18, and go not quite two and a half miles, just past the Polito Angus Farm, and turn right on State 570. In just over a mile, you'll see the Shinn Covered Bridge, built about 1886.

Stay with State 570 to Township 91, turn left, then turn left again on State 206, which takes you to State 555. At Bartlett, the Bartlett Restaurant on State 550 is a homey place to stop for breakfast or lunch; it's open every day. Leave Bartlett heading southeast on State 550, and immediately turn right on Township 77. At Township 61, turn right and you'll soon see the Henry Covered Bridge, built in 1892.

Stay on Township 61 until it brings you back to State 555. Turn left and proceed through Cutler, then watch for State 6, which is the next road after Township 238. Turn left on State 6 and you'll soon see the Root Covered Bridge.

Return to State 555 and continue south about a quarter of a mile, then turn left on State 3 to Veto, where you can turn left on State 339 to Barlow. At the fairgrounds here, see the Mill Branch Covered Bridge. Built in the 1830s, it's one of the oldest in the state. State 550 takes you back to Marietta.

Start early on a bright morning to drive this four-hour, self-guided tour of 35 scenic miles along the Little Muskingum River. You'll end up about an hour from Marietta just below Woodsfield. If you want a shorter tour, do only the first eight stops and return to Marietta on State 260. Note that the only gas, food, and drink along the route are at Myers General Store, which is open every day and offers canoe rentals. Recreation sites along the way have pit toilets but no drinking water.

From I-77, take State 7 south to the light, Acme Street, then turn right to Greene Street and right again. You'll be on State 26 for the next five miles, and here's where the Ohio Covered Bridge Scenic Byway begins. Turn right on County 333, and park at the south end of the bridge.

Ohio once had more than 2,000 covered bridges like this one. This one was built in 1878. Leaving the bridge, turn right on County 333, then right on State 26 and stay with this route northbound for the rest of the tour. Watch for the tour's second stop, which remembers Harley Warrick. He's the World War II veteran who, needing a job after the war, joined the team of painters who put the Mail Pouch Tobacco signs on barn sides. Now they're considered some of the Midwest's finest folk art. See how many you can spot in your travels.

When you reach the next stop, a covered bridge, you'll find a Forest Service parking area on the other side of the bridge (which has a clearance of 6'8" — RVs beware!) Near the parking lot, an oil pump display describes southern Ohio's oil and gas industry. It began not far from here in 1814 when diggers, searching for salt, struck oil. Except for lamplighting, oil didn't have a lot of uses in the days before motorcars. Some people called it devil's grease.

Returning to State 26 you'll come to a big white house on the left, the Hune House Inn. Built between 1885 and 1889, it was a boarding house and is now a bed-and-breakfast. Consider making an overnight stop here to break up your drive. The inn specializes in fine-arts retreats and workshops; resident artist is Thaddeus K. Brejwo.

Myers General Store, the next stop on the tour, is worth a stop even if you don't need anything. Since before the 20th century, it has been the only store for miles around. In earlier times, it housed the region's only public telephone, and also served as a post office. Leaving here after stocking up on food and drinks, you'll come to the Richard Covered Bridge on your right. Known as a "kissing" bridge because its long, dark interior was a good place to steal a kiss, this one was built in 1875. Continue now to Knowlton Bridge, which is on your right.

Turn right at the sign for Ring Mill and go about three miles to the tour's ninth stop, Ring Mill. The site dates to 1840, when a miller purchased the land, built a gristmill and sawmill, and put up a stone house for his family. Both mills lasted until the 1920s, when they were flooded. Continuing on your route, turn left at State 537, where you'll see a sign for the Lamping Homestead. Turn left, then after a mile, go left again on Township 307, then left into the parking lot. A homesteading family lived here early in Ohio's history. Their cemetery can still be seen nearby.

Your tour is now ended, so you can return to Marietta or continue up State 26 to Woodsfield, where you can follow State 800 to I-70.

For more information about area tourism, contact the Marietta/Washington County Convention & Visitors Bureau, 800-288-2577. For information about natural resources and outdoor recreation, contact National Forest, RR 1 Box 132, Marietta, OH 45750, 740-373-9055.

Leaving Marietta again on State 26 to the northeast, go just over six miles and turn right at the Hills United Methodist

Church, on Township 333. At once, you'll see the Hildreth Covered Bridge over the Little Muskingum River.

Go back to State 26, turn right, and drive through Sitka. On the hill on your right, you'll see a classic saltbox house; on your left, an ancient cemetery. Snaking through sycamore forests, the road is radiant with reds and yellows in fall and wreathed in greens from early spring through summer. As the road swoops and turns with the river, you'll catch glimpses of its emerald green color. It's said to be the cleanest watershed in the state.

At County 584, note the old Ewing Children's Home, built in 1858. Turn right if you're adventurous and have a car that can manage a steep, narrow, gravel road. It takes you past a country church and to a very old clifftop cemetery with a stunning view of the river valley below.

Continuing on State 26 to Moss Run, note all the piping and machinery along the road, nestled among the locust and black willow trees. Small, individual oil wells are still pumping, as they have been for decades. Gas wells throughout the region provide free cooking fuel and heat to lucky residents.

At Dart, note the swing bridge on your right. Because of frequent washouts, bridges are few and far between along this stretch of the Little Muskingum, so families put up these flimsy footbridges to give the children a shortcut to school.

The road winds through wildly beautiful scenery. Shale cliffs drip with little waterfalls, which, in winter, turn into shining icicles. Native hemlocks form the forests; bulging silos testify to the talent of farmers along rich bottomlands. The woods are floored with fern and trillium; the meadows with wildflowers.

Watch for the Lawrence Baptist Church and its adjoining cemetery. Just after the two-mile mark from here, turn left onto Township 34, where the Hune Covered Bridge, built in 1877, leads you to a beautiful park next to the babbling (and sometimes brimming) Little Muskingum. The area, which lies in yet another patch of the Wayne National Forest, is a canoe access point.

Just above the park, an 1830 home with its 1870 addition has been turned into a sunny hideaway set in fields of lavender, rhododendron, and lilies. In spring, hundreds of daffodils bloom here at Hune House Inn, a bed-and-breakfast. Shirley poppies have reseeded themselves, and wild roses bloom across the backyard. Retreats and nature seminars are sometimes scheduled here, so you might want to call and ask to be put on the mailing list.

Returning to State 26, turn right to pass through Wingett (pronounced Win Jet) Run. Continue on State 26, turn right on State 260, and right again on State 7 at New Matamoras. (The Grandview Tavern is a good place to have a crusty pizza.) This dramatic route follows the Ohio River and takes you back to Marietta. At the halfway mark, stop for a look at the Willow Island locks and dam. Just outside of Marietta, on County 20 in Reno, is Sandhill House, a Victorian farmhouse built in 1890.

For More Information

Marietta Convention and Visitors Bureau: 800-288-2577 or 614-373-5178, Website: www.rivertowns.org

The Lafayette (Marietta): 614-373-5522 or 800-331-9336

Classic Carriage Rides (departing from the Lafayette
    hotel on selected summer and fall evenings):
    614-667-3513

Becky Thatcher Restaurant and Lounge: 614-373-6033

Campus Martius Museum/Ohio River Museum (Marietta):
    614-373-3750 or 800-860-0145

Trolley Tours of Marietta (narrated tours of Marietta's
    attractions and history sites, April–October):
    614-374-2233

Betsey Mills dining room (Marietta): 614-373-3804
    (operated by the Blue Union Restaurant, 614-373-4604)

The Castle: 614-373-4180

The Levee House Cafe (Marietta): 614-374-2233

Henry Fearing House (Marietta): 614-373-9437

Harmar Station Historical Model Railroad Museum:
    614-374-9995

Attic Treasures (Marietta): 614-374-5343

Harper's Landing (Marietta): 614-373-3395

Buckley House Bed and Breakfast (Marietta): 614-373-3080 or
    888-282-5540

Lakeside Golf Course (Beverly): 614-984-4265

Bartlett Restaurant (Bartlett): 614-551-2838

Wayne National Forest (Marietta Unit): 614-373-9055

Valley Gem sternwheeler (narrated river cruises May–September
    and fall foliage cruises on October weekends):
    614-373-4130

Claire E. (authentic sternwheeler moored on the Muskingum):
  614-374-2233 or 614-374-3876

Myers General Store and Little Muskingum Canoe Livery:
  614-473-2258

Hune House Inn: 614-473-2039

Grandview Tavern (New Matamoras): 614-865-9907

13

Meigs County

Getting there: Our routes begin and end at Gallipolis, two hours (approximately 50 miles) south of Columbus via U.S. 23 and U.S. 35, and Marietta, 122 miles south of Cleveland via I-77.

Highlights: Breathtaking scenery along the Ohio River on State 124 and 338 between Pomeroy and Little Hocking. Heights and old homes, historic river towns and modern dams, Belpre, a view of Blennerhassett Island, and a patch of paradise time has passed by.

We suggest making this a two-day adventure, allowing time for hiking, sightseeing, or fishing. Don't let your gas tank or your stomach get too empty along this route. Facilities are few. This is a recreational route, not one to be traveled by anyone who is in a hurry.

Beginning at Gallipolis, head north on State 7 for the ride of a lifetime. Pause first in Pomeroy to see the stately old homes and a little museum at 144 Butternut Avenue. It's a gold mine for genealogical researchers. The village itself is a gem, nestled between high stone cliffs and the river.

Settled by the English, the community also attracted a lot of German immigrants, who settled here because the terrain reminded them of their home villages along the Rhine. Many of the homes along the main street are a century or more old.

At Pomeroy, turn south on State 124 and stay with it until you join Route 338. For more than 50 miles you'll switch and snake with the river, with towering cliffs on one side and water almost lapping at your hubcaps on the other. Watch for the *Delta Queen,* which might be seen anytime along the Ohio, her calliope wheezing pleasantly on the breeze.

At Portland, pause to shift from the 18th century into Civil War times, when Buffington Island was a battleground. The site of a prehistoric Indian mound, it's best known as the place where a bold Confederate general, John Hunt Morgan, met his Waterloo. Historic markers tell the story.

Hoping to draw Union troops away from eastern Tennessee, Morgan and 2,500 infantry troops infiltrated southern Ohio. After plundering Vinton in search of food and horses, they fought their way toward Chester, with the goal of escaping back across the Ohio and into West Virginia at the Buffington Island ford. Union troops cut them off there, killing 120 Rebels and taking 700 prisoners. Morgan fled north and was eventually captured in Columbiana County.

One of the many heroes of the event was Major David McCook, who, at 65, was eldest of the war's famous Fighting McCooks. He was wounded about a mile south of where the monument is today, and died on a boat that was taking him to Cincinnati for medical help.

Now a public park, Buffington Island is open year-round during daylight hours. Admission is free.

At Long Bottom continue north along the river five miles to Forked Run State Park and Shade River State Forest, where there is a marked hiking trail through native forest skittering with chubby squirrels, wild turkey, white-tailed deer, and red-tailed hawk.

Throughout the area, fishermen angle for abundant sauger, bass, catfish, bluegill, and crappie. Hot spots include Shade River, Old Town Creek, Ground Hog Creek, Old Portland Dam, Apple Grove Dam, Bellville Locks and Dam, and Racine Locks and Dam.

The 102-acre lake at Forked Run is stocked each year with thousands of trout and sauger. Launch ramps are found at Racine, Syracuse, Pomeroy, and Middleport. Forked Run State Park has camping, swimming, boating, canoe and paddleboat rental, as well as dockage on the Ohio.

Continue hugging the river road north to Hockingport, which slumbers through the winter but spills over in summer with happy boaters. If you love boating, boat camping, fishing, or just looking at boats, this is the place to join the crowds who set up their grills, start bonfires, and bond in boating camaraderie.

At Little Hocking, Stahl's Nursery and Christmas Shop makes a good place to stop and stroll the gardens. It's a complete garden center, and its year-round Christmas shop has 30 decorated trees and four rooms filled with goodies and gifts. It's open every day.

Continuing into Belpre, State 618 rims the river, but for a better view of Blennerhassett Island, take State 7 and watch for a Hardee's fast-food restaurant on your right. Its parking lot is the best vantage point in town for a look at Blennerhassett Island.

So far, we've resisted the temptation to talk about the many cities that are across the Ohio River in West Virginia, which are invariably a part of any tour of this area. They will be reserved for another book, *Country Roads of West Virginia*. But you may want to make a detour to Blennerhassett Island, in Parkersburg, West Virginia. If you do, take the toll bridge, U.S. 50, across to West Virginia and turn right on State 68 to Point Park, where ferries depart.

Ice Age hunters visited this island thousands of years ago, and in the 1760s it was the home of a Delaware Indian named

Nemacolin. George Washington came through in 1790 to look at Virginia lands he'd been given in exchange for his military service. Blennerhassett mansion, a grand manor surrounded by wilderness, attracted such well-known visitors as Henry Clay, Walt Whitman, George Rogers Clark, Johnny Appleseed, and even King Charles X of France.

Long a ruin, which added to its brooding air of mystery, the Blennerhassett mansion starred in one of history's most sinister intrigues. It was here, at the opulent mansion built by Irish aristocrat Harman Blennerhassett, that Aaron Burr took refuge after killing Alexander Hamilton in a duel. Rumors abounded that Burr and Blennerhassett were plotting to overthrow the government and set up their own empire.

Somebody tattled, and in 1806 the two were arrested for treason. Although they were never convicted, both men were ruined financially and a few years later the proud mansion burned down. It wasn't until 1973 that archaeologists excavated the foundations and work began on the exquisite replica you see today. The 500-acre island can be toured by bicycle or horse-drawn wagon, and the mansion is open for tours.

From the Hardee's lookout point, you can see the mansion and island with the naked eye or, for a closer look, use the coin-operated telescope. Below, on the river, there's a sprawling park and boat ramp within view of the island. Also in Belpre is the Lee Middleton Original Dolls factory at 1301 Washington Boulevard. Known to serious doll collectors around the world, handcrafted Middletons are made here in a gingerbread-facade "farmhouse." Factory tours are offered, and the factory outlet is a bargain-hunter's dream. Tour hours vary with the season, so call ahead. A factory outlet for Lloyd Middleton Dolls, which are made at a factory in Athens County, is found at 2005 Washington Boulevard, Belpre.

From here, it's a short hop into Marietta.

Leave Marietta southbound on State 7 along the river. Pass through Coolville, where a seminary for women opened in the 1860s, and continue into Chester, with its old homes and the oldest courthouse in the state, which dates to 1822. Next door is a schoolhouse that is about the same age.

If you want to stop in Chester for a self-guided fitness walk, it will take less than half a day. Three miles of wooded trails guide you over the hills and through the ravines to Morgan's Caves. For more information, contact the Meigs County Tourism Board.

Continuing on State 7, turn right on U.S. 33 North. We're on our way to one of those discoveries that make it worthwhile to leave the paving and venture onto gravel roads. Look for a left turn on County 19. The route, which is gravel, takes you through outcroppings of blue rock on forested hillsides, wooded gorges, and creekbeds flowing through riots of wildflowers. You're now in farm country as old as Ohio itself, in an area called Long Hollow. Again you'll note gas wells along the roads, providing free fuel to area residents.

The going gets more rugged as you turn left on Township 27A, passing even more isolated farm homes and traveling through rocky gorges and scrubby forests.

The log cabin at Crystal Creek on your right is available for rent by the night or the week. Built in 1830 and thoroughly modernized in 1993, it's set in a paradise of ponds and creeks, gorges and rocky caves. Walk up the abandoned roadbed to the waterfall, photographing ferns and morels along the way.

Stay on the road past the ruins of an old log corncrib, and it loops back to the highway. Go east on U.S. 33, then south on State 7, and you're back on course past the gorgeous heights of Laurel Cliff.

The ride south now on State 7 takes you through an area of soaring hillsides, many of them topped by homes that gaze out for miles over the Ohio River valley. Near Cheshire, note the big, black, snaking conveyor belt that serves the power company. A manmade wonder that shows up prominently on photographs from space satellites, it brings coal to these generators from mines many miles away.

Power created here serves much of the state. Because of the blasting and building hereabouts, it's locally called the Pity Me area, but it's only a short section in what has been a heady and memorable country drive.

For More Information

The Captain's House Inn (Middleport): 740-992-2101 or 800-445-8525

Stahl's Nursery and Christmas Shop (Little Hocking): 740-989-2271

Lee Middleton Original Dolls: 740-423-1481 or 800-133-7479

Lloyd Middleton Dolls: 740-423-8599 or 800-845-1845

Meigs County Chamber of Commerce (Pomeroy): 740-992-2239

Meigs County Tourism Board: 740-992-2239

Ohio River Cabins: 740-992-3785

Nature at Its Best Cabins: 740-992-5072

Crystal Creek Farm: 740-992-5351

14

Athens to Marietta

Getting there: Marietta is 122 miles from Columbus, 191 from Cincinnati, and 168 from Cleveland.

Highlights: Historic heartland farms, the site of the first library in the Northwest Territory, and the pleasures of yet another portion of the Wayne National Forest.

Our route covers a drive of less than 50 miles from Athens to Marietta via scenic State 550. We also suggest a longer route, which adds 22 miles and involves a little backtracking.

To get maximum pleasure from this drive, we suggest getting the one-hour audiocassettes issued by Sound Tracks, describing the route from Athens to Marietta or Marietta to Athens. They can be bought or rented from visitors bureaus in either city. The music accompaniment and interviews with old-timers who grew up in this area add immensely to the pleasure of the driving experience.

Leave Athens on State 550, which is one of the exits off U.S. 33 north of the city. The route follows Sugar Creek for three miles, and goes through an old mining town of the same name. Try to imagine it as it was in coal mining's glory days, when 100 lookalike company cottages were crammed into this tiny community. Their design was almost invariably a box topped by a four-sided, pyramid roof.

Until 1906, the Hocking valley supplied more coal than any other region of the state. During World War I, seven million tons a year were mined here by men whose simple homes have long since disappeared.

From the valley, the view of the high ridges is a new pleasure as you round each corner. It was along these ridges, warmed by the nighttime rise of warm air out of the bottomlands, that acres of peaches and apples once abounded. Still rich in orchards, most of them apple, this part of Ohio was once famous for its peach brandy. One of Gallipolis's first settlers, in fact, made his fortune in peach brandy. He's remembered at the Stowaway Restaurant there, with recipes that still feature peach brandy as an ingredient.

All along State 550, you'll see classic farm homes in the style known as the "I" house, because it was the style used by most settlers in the "I" states (Illinois, Indiana, and Iowa) as soon as they were able to build something better than their original log cabins. Traditionally, the house was a rectangle with five windows across the second floor and four windows, with a door in the middle, on the first floor. Chimneys on each end served fireplaces on both floors.

In time, wealthier farmers and merchants were able to follow changing tastes, so they built Victorian homes with their towers, turrets, elaborate cutwork, and trim on trim. This in turn gave way to another home style, the Sears Roebuck kit house, with its easy adaptability to even more modern needs—central heating and plumbing.

Almost all the history of Ohio architecture can be seen along this ribbon of highway: a few log cabins, some rows of rubber-stamp miner's cottages, "I" houses, Victoriana, and more modern homes, many of them built from the Sears Roebuck mail-order kits, which date roughly to 1910–1930.

At State 690, turn right and you'll follow Mush Run for not quite two miles. Stay with 690 at the old cemetery, where Mush Run Road takes off to the left. On your right are patches of private land and pieces of the Wayne National Forest. Two miles later, old Canaan Church and cemetery can be seen as you come to U.S. 50. Turn left into Canaanville, once a busy railroad town.

U.S. 50 roughly follows the Hocking River and includes glimpses of river scenery, old houses, and tiny cemeteries. Watch for the left turn on State 329 after about four miles. It takes you through Guysville, a charming old community where the Ohio Hempery sells legal hemp products including trendy clothing, hemp oil, bags, and accessories.

Between Guysville and Stewart you'll pass an ambitious academy, one of the many high-quality schools that were established in the Northwest Territory by settlers from the Northeast. Graduates of Harvard and Yale, they wanted the hardships of frontier life to stop at the schoolhouse door. Miller Academy opened in 1841, and, because most students had to board here, the campus included the main school building as well as residential cottages. The remains of this still-impressive spread are now the Red Bird Ranch.

Proceed into Stewart if you are a plant fancier. The Glasshouse Works Greenhouses on Church Street in this tiny town are not hard to find. They are the only "tourist attraction" in town, and they are known worldwide. Here, partners Tom Winn and Ken Frieling have collected the rarest plants from all over the world, and they propagate and sell them. One of their goals has been to list in their catalog every variegated houseplant that exists.

Backtracking from Stewart toward Guysville on State 329, turn right on County 84, which follows Miller Run to the old hamlet of New England. Then turn left on County 34 (you're now on Mush Run Road), which takes you back to a right turn on State 690. The detour has taken you through some of the county's oldest and most authentic farm and mining territory, and now you're back on State 550 en route to Marietta.

Coming into Amesville at the County 18 intersection, Amesville Cemetery was known by settlers by the unlovely name Mud Suck. On some maps, it's spelled Mud Sock, but you get the idea. Sweet-smelling cedars were brought in by early settlers to scent these boggy lowlands. To today's traveler, the damp makes things all the more beautiful because the bottomlands beam with moisture-loving wildflowers, scrubby sumac, and willows bending low over streamlets that glint silver in the sun.

Because early Amesville settlers were well-educated Easterners, many of them Revolutionary War veterans with their families, founding a library became one of their first priorities. They paid for books in pelts, the only "money" they had.

Minutes of the membership meeting in 1804 reflect that 51 books had been bought for $68.45½, minus a discount of $7.07½, plus a charge of $12.12 for carriage and paper. By 1850, Amesville's Coonskin Library had a collection of 235 precious volumes.

The site of this first library, which originally was a portable book collection housed, in turn, in the homes of townspeople, is seen as you enter Amesville. A marker was erected by the Daughters of the American Revolution as a reminder that, despite its homespun nickname, this was a library created by literate settlers, not by ignorant backwoodsmen.

In 1976 some of the original books went up for auction, one of which was purchased by Ohio University for $180. That's a lot of bucks. The term "bucks," incidentally, originated when a buckskin in these parts was worth a dollar and bought an entire book.

The more time you have to nose around Amesville, the more discoveries you can make. One of ours was the home and workshop of Randall K. Fields, whose shingle next to the Methodist Church reads Klaerfields Nursery. Fields sells nursery plants, but he's also a brilliant artist and furniture crafts-man whose original designs sell for $2,000 or more. If you're an Ohioan, shop the plant nursery for trees, shrubs, and perennials. The Fields start most of their plants themselves, so you're assured of getting plantings suitable for the Ohio climate.

Intrigued with its symmetry and engineering perfection, Fields began with the classic Windsor chair design. Then the art major in him rebelled at regimentation, and he began to add color and new form without departing from the integrity of the inherently strong and durable chair design. Stop in dur-ing business hours and he'll talk to you about plants or custom-made furniture or both.

Continuing east on State 550, you'll see a yellow farmhouse just past State 329. It has been occupied by the same family since 1817.

We continue to follow the river valleys into Lathrop, where at one time the Black Diamond coal mine employed 100 men. The community, which lies just off State 550 on Township 512, had 20 or more company houses, a store, and grander homes for the mine manager and the superintendent. Only the superintendent's house remains.

Stay on State 550, which makes a sharp right at Sharps-burg. Bartlett, once a Quaker community, was another of Ohio's many stops on the Underground Railroad. Slaves who crossed the Ohio River at Hockingport knew they could find shelter and directions to their next refuge here.

Look closely at the barns along the route. Most of them have some small design quirk, such as a star-shaped vent at the peak. These were the trademarks of the carpenter crews who built them. Often, they symbolized the workmen's masonic orders.

Near Layman, note the splendid brick "I" house with its quoined corners. At Barlow, a roadside rest area gives you a chance to pull over, step out of the car, and breathe deeply of sweet Ohio country air with its clovers and apple blossoms in springtime or musky leaves and dried cornstalks in autumn. This is the home of the county fairgrounds, and there's an old-fashioned general store on your left.

Continuing on State 550, you'll see stranded stands of stone pillars from time to time. They're the remains of the Marietta & Cincinnati Railroad, which served this area from 1857 to the early 1900s. Only the stone trestles remain, but at one time the town of Tunnel had—you guessed it—a three-mile tunnel. Grindstone quarries operated here until the 1960s.

Approaching Marietta, you'll pass what was once the community of Pinehurst. Here the Silver Globe Manufacturing Company still makes the gazing globes that seemed to grace every front yard in the United States in the 1930s and 40s. The globes, which never lost their popularity, are making a comeback nationwide, and decorators are snapping them up for indoor, as well as outdoor, use. The company, still family owned and still making the globes by hand, is one of only two such manufacturers in the country.

For More Information

Athens County Convention and Visitors Bureau: 740-592-1819
   or 800-878-9767

Ohio Hempery: 740-662-4367

Glasshouse Works Greenhouses (Stewart): 740-662-2142

Randall K. Fields and Klaerfields Nursery (Amesville):
   740-448-2321

15

Athens to Logan

Getting there: Straddling the Hocking River in southeastern Ohio, Athens is the home of Ohio University. The city is 73 miles from Columbus; 142 miles from Cincinnati, via the scenic, multilane Appalachian Highway (U.S. 32); and 201 miles from Cleveland.

Highlights: A county of contrasts: pockets of Appalachian poverty, deserted mining towns, parks and trails for the outdoorsman, historic mansions, plus the pace and pizzazz of Ohio University.

Athens is a small city, but its size doubles when more than 27,000 students swarm into town. Founded in 1804, the year after Ohio became a state, Ohio University was the first university chartered in the Northwest Territory. The frontier school opened in 1808 with one building, one professor, and three students.

The campus enriches the community in many ways. One is the cosmopolitan, international ambience it adds. Another is its many special events featuring nationally known artists, authors, and lecturers. The Kennedy Museum of American Art in Lin Hall houses an outstanding collection of southwestern Native American art and artifacts, including the sand-painting designs of six complete Navajo chants. Third is the campus itself, a tourist attraction that can be enjoyed on many levels, from architecture to botany.

Exiting State 682 north at Richland Avenue, you'll cross the Hocking River and immediately spot the university's visitors center, housed in a log cabin on your left. Stop for maps and guidance and a look at the cabin.

Built by Silas Bingham, who was sent here by the Ohio Company in 1797 to arrange for land for the university, the house dates to at least 1803 and probably earlier. Because early elections and council meetings were held here, it is considered the county's first courthouse, too. The structure has been moved, improved, sided, cut up, partitioned, and renovated many times over the centuries, but the poplar logs are inescapably cloaked in history.

Although a visit to the log cabin is fascinating, you'll be better prepared for your campus tour if you also write ahead for information from Ohio University, Athens, OH 45701-2979. Request walking-tour maps of the campus and any other information related to your own special interests.

If you can't find on-street parking, use the municipal parking garage at the corner of Washington and College streets. Guided tours of the campus last about an hour, starting at the Office of Admissions, Chubb Hall, at 10:00 A.M. and 2:00 P.M. Monday through Friday, and Saturday at noon.

Points of interest on the stately, tree-shaded campus include the Wolfe Garden, which is in the shape of the state of Ohio; the 45-foot Soldiers' Monument, built in 1893 to honor Civil War dead; and countless grand buildings going back to the early 19th century.

For the country-roads traveler, the tree tour of the College Green is a good way to get acquainted with the full range of Ohio trees you'll encounter in the wild. It's an outstanding arboretum, planted with at least 50 types of trees, from ash and beech to witch hazel and yellowwood. Request the self-guided tour map from the address listed above. It shows what species are where, and also cross-indexes the trees alphabetically so you can find, say, a weeping cherry or a white fringeberry to add to your tree-spotting collection.

Athens was founded as a home for Ohio University, so the small town grew up around it. Court Street in the heart of the campus, with its galleries and boutiques, is an especially happy hunting ground for shoppers.

Dewey's at 23 West Union Street is a chic shop where you can have a sundae, stock up on Godiva chocolates, or sit in the dining room and choose from a large, varied menu.

A must for gift and souvenir seekers is the Log Cabin Gift Shop.

The route northwest from Athens on U.S. 33 takes you along the Hocking River on a road that was, in parts, the old Hocking Valley Canal. Our next checkpoint is Nelsonville, where we enjoyed one of those surprises that make travel an adventure.

Most people zip through the town on U.S. 33, seeing what appears to be only a grubby old railroad town. Actually the present-day highway was once the canal bed, so the buildings here were *meant* to be commercial and utilitarian. Only a block to the north are the proud old residential streets and a town square so charming it was used in the filming of the movie *Mischief*.

Before leaving U.S. 33, however, stop at the Brooks Shoe Company, home of the famous Rocky Boot. Factory tours are offered on weekdays by appointment; the factory outlet, laden with bargains, is open Monday through Saturday, 9:00 A.M. to 7:00 P.M., and Sunday, 11:30 A.M. to 5:30 P.M. The building is on your left on U.S. 33, Canal Street. You'll see its huge murals well in advance; park in the rear.

Turning north on Hocking Street takes you into a quiet neighborhood of gracious Victorian homes. Look high to the hill on your right and you'll see the world's largest freestanding illuminated cross, a sight you may want to visit again after dark.

Turn right on Columbus Street and stop at the town square. Surrounding the open square are buildings, including the historic Stuart's Opera House, where the nation's top professional entertainers "trod the boards" from 1879 to 1924. Presidential candidates including Taft, McKinley, and Harding always stopped at the Dew Hotel to give speeches from its balcony. Built in 1839, it has been restored and once again rings with fine music and theater. The fountain, dedicated in 1904, has been a landmark ever since—sometimes filled with flowers, sometimes with water, and, during one whimsical era, with an alligator.

Now drive east to 32 Columbus, where you'll see the Cable House, built in 1838. On Washington Street, the next block north, note the First Presbyterian Church at number 69. It was built in 1873 of the locally fired bricks that formed so many of the homes and streets of Athens County.

One of the oldest homes in the area is at 87 Fayette Street, a block south of Columbus. It was built in 1814 and has been moved three times. If you want to continue out Fort Street a few blocks and watch for the cemetery on your left, you'll find the grave of Daniel Nelson, founder of Nelsonville, midway up the hill just past the black post. Also buried here are many Civil War soldiers.

The Hocking Valley Scenic Railway, now a tourist attraction, is all that is left today of a major transportation network that brought 200 trains a day here to haul away 200,000 tons of locally mined coal. The area bulged with brickyards, as many as 90 coal mines, and industries of all kinds.

The train departs the depot, which is at the center of town at U.S. 33 and the Hocking Parkway, on weekends, Memorial Day through October. The route sometimes parallels sites you'll see on country roads, and sometimes takes you into more remote territory, so it's an excellent counterpoint to your driving tour.

The train makes special runs with the seasons, including a fall color trip and Santa trains in December. Offered in-season are a 10-mile round-trip to Diamond and a 25-mile round-trip to Logan. Reservations are recommended.

On your right, pass the area's one remaining brick factory, a charming chapel on the left, then Dee's Diner. Also very popular is the Coffee Cup on the west side of Nelsonville, with an enormous menu of 150 items including vegetarian choices. Design your own meal. It's open 6:00 A.M. to 8:00 P.M. Monday through Saturday and Sunday 8:00 A.M. to 6:00 P.M. Now watch for a left turn to Haydenville, which lies just off the main road.

Keeping in mind that this is a private, residential street, drive the three-block-long main street of this ghostlike community and ponder the years, not so long ago, when many citizens of Athens County were housed in company towns like this.

Typically in such towns there was a company store, post office, a school, housing for workers, and a grander home where the mine superintendent lived. Not so typical is the larger size, and more elegant—if somewhat weird-looking—construction of the homes Mr. Hayden built for his workers. Made of locally made brick and tile, they were given individual features to avoid the lookalike sameness of other company towns. When taken to see this unusual settlement, design pioneer Buckminster Fuller is said to have dubbed its style "sewer pipe gothic."

Throughout southeastern Ohio, you'll see similar communities, most of them much more ramshackle and many of them abandoned. Even the most modest villages, however, had a school, usually well built of brick or stone, a company store, and a church.

Return to U.S. 33 and continue west for only a quarter mile, watching for a right turn on State 595. It's a switchy, winding, green stretch of road that takes you through yet another piece of Wayne National Forest. Note the many trailheads seen on both sides of the road and stop for a short hike on any of the marked trails. A patchwork of lands that have been bought by the government as they became available, the forest is not one plot but a great many, here and there, throughout several counties in southern Ohio.

After about five enjoyable and scenic miles, just across the Perry County line you'll come to another of the old mining towns, New Straitsville. At one time it was the moonshine capital of the Midwest. On the way, you'll pass through Greendale, where you'll see a few miners' homes. Just before crossing State 278, note the old church and cemetery. The road leads to Carbon Hill, still another of the old mining towns.

One other, by the way, is not on our route but you may want to look it up if you remember the famous Millfield mine disaster. A marker honors the 79 people who died there on November 5, 1930. Just as Ohioans remember where they were at the moment President Kennedy was shot, many of them also remember the exact moment when they received word of the Millfield tragedy or the collapse of the Silver Bridge. Millfield is north of Athens on State 13. We'll stay on State 595.

A hotbed of labor strife throughout the last of the coal-mining heydays here, New Straitsville was in the national news in 1930 when its striking miners set fire to a coal car, sent it into the mine, and started a fire that burned underground and unquenchable until the 1970s.

Meanwhile, they set up stills in abandoned mines and sold high-grade 'shine to thirsty bargain seekers, who came from miles around. One story goes that a booze-buyer who was here on his first shopping expedition asked a bystander where he might buy liquor in town. To his amazement, the local pointed to the Methodist church. While the stranger was pondering this, the local chap added laconically, "That there is the only place in town where you *can't* buy moonshine." The little community is still the site of an annual Moonshine Festival in May.

At New Straitsville, turn left on State 93, which leads west, then south through more of the Wayne National Forest, through Gore and into Logan. Along the route, you'll seem lost in times gone by as you pass remains of railroad spurs, coal tipples, mining villages, country stores that have seen better days, churches struggling to stay alive, and churches and schools that have already died.

At Logan, continue south on State 93, where you'll see two covered bridges before reaching McArthur. The Cox Bridge, just south of State 56, was built in 1884; the Tinker (or Bay) Bridge is at the Vinton County Junior Fairgrounds, one and a half miles north of McArthur. It dates to 1876.

From McArthur, turn east on U.S. 50 for six miles, then turn left on State 278, which takes you through the dramatic scenery of the Lake Hope area and the Zaleski State Forest. You'll eventually emerge on U.S. 33 just west of Nelsonville. Now you're only about 40 miles from Columbus. Or, return to Athens and continue with the routes described in the next chapter.

For More Information

Athens County Convention and Visitors Bureau: 740-592-1819 or 800-878-9767

Greater Logan County Area Convention and Tourist Bureau: 937-599-2016 or 888-564-2626

Ohio University Visitors Center: 740-593-2097

Log Cabin Gift Shop: 740-594-4387

The Albany House (Albany): 740-698-6311

Brooks Shoe Company (Nelsonville): 740-753-3130

Stuart's Opera House (Nelsonville): 740-753-1924

Hocking Valley Scenic Railway: 513-335-0382 or 614-753-9531

16

Logan and the Hocking Hills

Getting there: Start at Logan, which is an hour (about 40 miles) east of Columbus on U.S. 33. A tour of the Hocking Hills covers 50 miles or less.

Highlights: The historic community of Logan, rambling country roads, and the ruggedly beautiful terrain of the Hocking Hills.

In the last chapter, we went through Logan southbound on State 93. Its chief east-west road is U.S. 33 from Columbus to Athens.

Another Ohio picture-book community with its classic town square, obligatory Civil War monument, and Schempp House Museum, operated by the Hocking County Historical Society, Logan was already a prosperous farming community when the first canal boat came through here on the Hocking Canal in 1840. The first train arrived in 1869. The death of the canal system and the downturn in rail transport put an end to the boom years, leaving only the small-town loveliness.

If you plan to pause in Logan for a walking tour, write ahead to the Logan-Hocking Chamber of Commerce, Box 838, Logan 43138 and request a brochure. It describes two routes, with descriptions of points of interest along the way. Drive both routes in an hour or so, or take both routes on foot, with lunch in between at Bush's, a homey and unpretentious place at 428 East Front Street. Or stop at LF's Cafe in the Marketplace on Main, a gallery of retail shops at 4 Main Street.

Walking or driving the historic area, you'll pass two dozen classic buildings including the old stagecoach inn at Main and Walnut, built in 1867. An even older house, dating to 1847, is at 272 West Main Street. Most of the sites of note are Greek Revival, Queen Anne, and Italianate. An interesting departure is the Spanish House at 3 Gallagher Avenue, built in 1929 at the height of the fashion for Mediterranean architecture.

The Schempp House Museum complex of historical buildings, including an 1881 home, is at Hunter and Culver Streets. It's open Saturday afternoon from late May into October, and other times by appointment. Among its displays is a steam automobile invented by Henry Lutz and built in Logan in 1898.

Continuing south on State 664, on the way to Hocking Hills State Park, there's a KOA on your left about five miles south of town. If you camp, this 80-acre campground is an ideal headquarters for visiting local attractions. Pets are welcome, and horseback riding, golf, and fishing are nearby. In another mile, find the Wildwood General Store, which is a last chance to get cold drinks and other supplies for your stay in the park. The store is open every day and also sells firewood, beer and wine, and handmade crafts.

Once inside the park, it's best to follow signs to the various areas: trails, dining lodge, and waterfalls, depending on your interests, physical abilities, and the time available. You can take an easy hike, a vigorous trek, or a rapelling expedition; pitch a tent, book a night in a cabin, or simply stay for the day and a picnic. The terrain is stunning. Worn deeply hollow by centuries of water flow and wind erosion, cliffsides have been turned into caves, shady glens, and awesome overhangs.

The trail to Ash Cave, named because ashes from Indian fires were found here, not only is one of the most scenic, but also is wheelchair accessible. During wet seasons, usually winter and spring, there's a splashy, 90-foot waterfall. The entire trail from Ash Cave to Cedar Falls is a bracing three-mile walk. If you are good for another three miles, take the trail from Cedar Falls to Old Man's Cave, named for a hermit who lived here after the Civil War. For fishermen, access to Rose Lake is from a parking area on State 374.

The bedrock was deposited here 350 million years ago, a delta in the warm sea that covered Ohio before the glaciers came. Seven thousand years ago, a culture called the Adena people came here to take shelter in the hollowed-out rock surrounded by sweet, sheltering hemlocks. By the time the first white settlers arrived, the Adena were gone and the area was roamed by tribes we call the Wyandot, Delaware, and Shawnee.

A gristmill was built at Cedar Falls and a powder mill near Rock House in 1835, where a house-shaped rock formation can be seen in the cliff. By the turn of the century the caves were already a tourist attraction. The Forest View Restaurant and Conference Center in Hocking Hills State Park is the perfect place to eat while gazing through the window wall into the majestic woodland.

Located on State 374 on the rim of the park, just 2.5 miles from South Bloomingville, The Inn at Cedar Falls is set on 60 acres of meadows strewn with wildflowers, wooded hillsides, and blackhand sandstone sculpted by Mother Nature. Call ahead to book a room or a meal. Ellen Grinsfelder, innkeeper and chef, and her late mother renovated an 1840 log cabin, which forms the core of the inn. Nine new rooms, each with private bath, have been added, and the inn also has two meeting rooms with woodburning stoves. Ellen also offers six secluded log cabins, each on its own plot of two acres or more. Built from logs salvaged from homes built in the early

1800s, the cozy cabins are fully furnished, complete with cooking facilities, to accommodate 2 to 4 people. Light your gas log or sit on the private porch in your own Ohio wilderness world.

Also available for rent by the night year-round is Fernwood, a log home in the woods 2.5 miles off Route 33 and three miles from Cantwell Cliffs. It sleeps two in the bedroom and two more in the loft, and has fireplace, fully equipped modern kitchen, central heat and air, hot tub, telephone, television, and VCR. Firewood is furnished October 1–April 1.

Leave the park northbound on State 374 and turn onto Big Pine Road through Conkles Hollow Nature Reserve. Get out of your car and walk around to appreciate nature's sculpture in the rock formations and to look for rare plants. Wild orchids are in the area, but only a privileged few ever find one.

If your travels take you north out of Logan on U.S. 33, jog west on County 34, which is north of State 180, to find Catch the Wind, a whimsical shop where Donna Voelkel sells country accessories, Christmas collectibles, and hand-painted gifts. The shop is open Wednesday through Sunday 10:00 A.M. to 5:00 P.M.

Return to State 374 and turn right to pass through Rock House, which has a picnic area. At the corner with State 180, Rockhouse Station sells fuel, ice, basic supplies, and all the Amish favorites including handmade brooms and homemade jams, cheese, noodles, jellies, and sausages.

Stay with State 374, which pretzels around to show you the Cantwell Cliffs. You'll pass Buck Run Studio, a country shop spilling over with quilts, baskets, folk art, weavings, and other gifts. Hours vary, so call ahead. Stay on State 374, which takes you back to U.S. 33, only a few miles northwest of Logan, where you started.

For More Information

Athens County Convention and Visitors Bureau: 740-592-1819
or 800-878-9767

Hocking County Tourism Association: 740-385-9706 or
800-HOCKING, Website: www.hockinghills.com

Bush's (Logan): 740-385-7639

Marketplace on Main: 740-385-3024

Schempp House Museum: 740-385-4034 or 740-385-2707

Wildwood General Store: 740-385-7934

Hocking Hills State Park: 740-385-6841, 740-385-6836, or
800-HOCKING

Forest View Restaurant and Conference Center: 740-385-6495

The Inn at Cedar Falls: 740-385-3024 or 800-65-FALLS

Fernwood: 740-385-4630

Catch the Wind: 740-385-0552

Buck Run Studio: 740-385-5560

Grandma Fay's: 740-385-9466

17

Another World

Gallia County

Getting there: From Huntington, West Virginia, and I-64, cross the river and turn right on State 7 toward Gallipolis. At Eureka, catch a glimpse of the massive Gallipolis Locks and Dam, the first roller dam in the United States. From Cleveland, take I-77 south to Marietta, then continue south along the river on State 7. From Columbus, take State 23 south, go east on State 35 to State 7, and stay with it into Gallipolis. Gallipolis (pronounced gallup police) is about 85 miles southeast of Columbus and about 100 miles east of Cincinnati.

Highlights: Cliffy hills, villages older than Ohio itself, French settlers and Welsh miners; through Patriot to Rio Grande and into Vinton, where Morgan's Raiders burned the Raccoon Creek Bridge during the Civil War.

W e recommend an audiocassette tour called Country Roads. The two-hour tape can be purchased or rented from the visitors center, and it's a delightful companion to this country roads tour. It describes the route mile by mile, and accompanies each section with appropriate music, interviews with old-timers, and historical anecdotes.

Winters are mild in the river bottoms, with the occasional ice or snowstorm preceded by a few days of rainy gloom and followed by clearing skies of incredible blue. Depending on what kind of winter it has been, the river can be fractious in spring, but it's always interesting and alive—so alive that in March 1913 the river reached a crest of 66.5 feet and swamped hundreds of homes. Gallipolis had been built on a 50-foot escarpment high above the waters, but that was not quite high enough. The Ohio flooded even worse in this area in 1937, but flood control projects appear to have stemmed disasters of this magnitude.

Summer means baseball, canoeing the creeks, hiking the gorgeous gorges. Found along Raccoon Creek are the rare reflexed umbrella sedge and tufts of violets. Fall brings color to cliffs, hillsides, dooryards, and parks as hickory trees turn liquid gold, maples and sourwood scream red, and dogwood bursts with red drupes.

Bow hunters stalk deer, turkey grouse run for cover, and muzzle-loader season opens. After Labor Day, the pace slows and the locals begin closing up shop, so it's best to check ahead for room availability, open and closing times, and special events.

This is Ohio's Appalachia, geographically as well as economically. Scenery is rugged, hills higher and steeper, forests thicker, and services more sparse. We are now in the area of some of Ohio's most beautiful and remote country roads. Unlike the neat north-south, east-west grids of flatter parts of the state, these roads intertwine as they thread through hills and wind along rivers.

The riverside road is State 7. Keep in mind that the Ohio River runs east and west through much of southern Ohio but north and south through most of Gallia County, which is disorienting to some seat-of-the-pants navigators. You may have to navigate by a compass or the sun, but not by the river. The main east-west road through the county is U.S. 35, which ends at the river at the landmark Silver Memorial Bridge.

Because this area is located so remotely in a deep corner of southeastern Ohio, we chose to begin and end our route in Gallipolis.

If you're entering the area from the north on State 7 or from the east on U.S. 35, you'll find the Silver Memorial Bridge at the northern edge of Gallipolis. Today it's just another busy route to the West Virginia side of the river, but think back for a moment to December 15, 1967, when the original Silver Bridge, half a mile from this one, cracked, buckled, and catapulted 37 vehicles into the icy Ohio.

Forty-six people died, so suddenly that one victim was found the next day still grasping the dollar bill he was about to use to pay the driver of the cab in which he was riding. Throughout the area, people today still remember what they were doing at the exact moment when they heard this stunning news. Even on the most raw days, you'll see people at the memorial marker, reading the names of the dead.

Pause at the park that now overlooks the site to read the memorial markers and to study an eye bar like the one that failed, causing the collapse. The park offers plenty of parking, rest rooms, a picnic area, and a fine river overlook.

Heading south on State 7 toward Gallipolis, note the dramatic Cliffside Golf Course on your right. Then, for a short detour into a moment in Gallipolis history, turn right past the golf course on Mill Creek Road and you'll soon see Haskins Memorial Park. The three stone water towers here, built in 1892 by Ohio Penitentiary prisoners, and a fine sandstone building were part of the Ohio Hospital for Epileptics. Before that, the site was Camp Carrington and dated to Civil War times.

The park offers year-round tennis, basketball, a playground, picnicking, and an Olympic-size swimming pool, which is open Memorial Day through Labor Day.

Return to State 7, turn right, pass State 160, and, when State 7 jogs right on Sycamore, go straight as the road becomes First Avenue, along the river to the City Park.

Ohio is known for its classic, almost Disneyesque city squares and picturesque main streets, many of them beautifully restored and still the hearts of their communities. However, we'll go out on a limb and claim this one in Gallipolis as the most beautiful. Because it was an enormous depot during the Civil War, the green space here is twice as large as that of most town squares. Shops and neighborhoods face the park, which is centered by an ornate white bandstand. Strolling its paths, think back to 1790, when the first French settlers landed here by boat and scrambled up the riverbank.

Park anywhere on the perimeter of the park and set out on foot. The Ohio Valley Visitors Center is at 45 State Street, the street that forms the park's eastern edge. Its northern border is Second Avenue; its western, Court Street. It's best to write ahead for the brochure describing the walking/driving tour for this history-packed area.

In the park itself, note the bandstand, which dates to 1876. A doughboy statue was built after World War I, and another memorial honors the 66 people who died when a passing riverboat brought the dreaded "yellow jack" to Gallipolis in 1878.

Yellow fever had broken out aboard a sternwheeler, which began to put sick men ashore at each port. When word leaped ahead of the boat, revealing that the disease was aboard, she was refused docking at town after town. Then a rocker arm snapped, and the helpless boat drifted back with the current, coming to rest at Gallipolis. The monument to the dead is topped with a replica of that fateful rocker arm, which started the whole tragedy by bringing the fever to Gallipolis.

Along First Avenue, there is a three-story, yellow-brick house, circa 1896; a Queen Anne house built in 1910 at 200

First Avenue; and a Federal-style home at 212, which dates to 1840. The Victorian house at 224 was built around 1840. The neoclassical masterpiece at 228, built about 1850, has white-marble fireplaces and a walnut staircase.

Most of the houses on Court Street are even older. The house at 1 Court dates to 1811; the house at 11 Court was built in 1820 as a home and shop. At 13 Court, the Federal-style brick building is said to have been the home of a counterfeiter.

You can hardly go wrong by continuing to walk up and down the streets between Cedar and Grape, Fourth and First. Found near the confluence of the Ohio and Kanawha Rivers, which were some of America's first highways, Gallipolis spreads street after quiet street of well-kept historic homes.

In what was one of the earliest of America's long list of land scams, a group of 500 Frenchmen—most of them fleeing the busy guillotine of the French Revolution—bought land from the Scioto (pronounced sigh-OH-tow) Company and set sail for the New World in 1790.

They arrived to discover that their land deeds were worthless, but they found a sympathetic ear in President Washington, whose generals well remembered the Marquis de Lafayette's part in our own revolution. A village of log cabins and blockhouses was hastily built along the Ohio River for the refugees, and the community became Gallipolis, or City of the Gauls, in October 1790.

Many of the French noblemen drifted away. Bred to the soft life of servants and silks, they were unable to handle life on the unforgiving frontier. Those few who had grit and guile stayed, worked hard enough to buy their land a second time—this time legally—and put roots deep into the Ohio soil.

By 1819, the little settlement merited a cozy, three-story brick inn, which today is a first-class museum, and new settlers began to pour in. Known as Our House, the tavern hosted General Lafayette during his triumphant tour of America in 1825; his visit here is commemorated each May. The museum, which displays one of the Marquis de Lafayette's coats in a glass case, is open daily from Memorial Day through Labor Day, except Monday. Admission is charged.

The Berthelot Home at 449 First Avenue, built in 1802, is the oldest frame building in town. The Federal Row House at 413–417 First Avenue was built by one of the original French 500 in the European style, with shops on the ground floor and the merchants' living quarters upstairs.

At 530 First Avenue find the French Art Colony Regional Multi-Arts Center housed in a graceful, 1855–56 Greek Revival mansion, wrapped in a spacious porch accented with white pillars. Stop in to see the galleries and special exhibits, Tuesday through Friday from 10:00 A.M. to 3:00 P.M., Sunday from 1:00 to 5:00 P.M., plus additional hours during special events.

Also the scene of special events is the Ariel Theatre, built as an Odd Fellows lodge in 1895. Later it became an opera house. Now the building, with its mellow oak woodwork and outstanding acoustics, provides an elegant backdrop for concerts and community theater. It's also the home of the Ohio Valley Symphony, a rare treasure for a community of this size. It's at 424 Second Avenue.

Housed in the old G. C. Murphy dime store building at 350 Second Avenue is French City Mall Crafts and Antiques. Local people create the delightful, unique handmade items and are on hand to chat with you about their antiques. Hours vary seasonally, so call the Ohio Valley Visitors Center of Gallia County for information.

At 401, note the old Park Central Hotel, built in 1883 on the site of a house and mall constructed here in 1840 and incorporated into the hotel structure.

If you enjoy browsing old cemeteries, drive east on Third Avenue and go left on Pine a few blocks to Pine Street Cemetery, which was established around 1790. The most interesting monuments are those of the original French settlers, and that of Congressman Vinton, for whom Ohio's Vinton County was named in 1850. The visitors center provides a map showing the location of other graves of interest. They include Marie Boben Menager (1772–1854), who was said to have once been wooed by Napoleon Bonaparte; Dr. Jonas Safford (1763–1843), a Revolutionary War veteran who came to Gallipolis to practice dentistry; Adelaide Baguet, one of the early French settlers who was captured by Indians; and Charles Duteil, one of the French 500 who is said to have killed the only buffalo seen in Gallia County. The doughboy statue in Public Square honors John C. Oliver, who died at the age of 18 in World War I and is buried in this cemetery.

Cemeteries in this part of Ohio have a surprising number of Revolutionary War veterans, especially officers. In order to claim the lands deeded to them for war service, the veterans had to come here in person. As a result, many stayed on until their deaths.

The beloved old Stowaway Restaurant is now Le Marquis Bistro and Lounge, at 300 Second Avenue at the Court Street intersection. It was originally named in honor of Francois Valodin (1765–1826), who stowed away on one of the ships that brought the original French 500 to this area. He was discovered and, as was the practice with stowaways, was indentured to a hotelkeeper in Virginia to pay for his passage. A year later he was freed, found his way to Gallipolis, and became one of the wealthiest men in town through hard work and the brewing of a fabulous peach brandy made from local fruits. The restaurant retains its wonderful French flair.

If you're more in the mood for a quick snack, try Remo's, which is just around the corner from Le Marquis. Remo, who is a local legend, serves nothing but cold pop and hot dogs with his secret Italian sauce. A lunch spot favorite of the downtown business crowd is the City Perk at 42 Court Street. It has a broad choice of sandwiches, soups, pastries, and coffees.

When you're ready to leave Gallipolis, take State 141 west and turn left at the entrance to Fortification Hill, where cannon were mounted during the Civil War. The highest bluff in this area, it looks out over Gallipolis, the Ohio River, and across to West Virginia. Have a picnic in this leafy park and stroll through Mound Hill Cemetery. Buried here is O. O. McIntyre, a local boy whose fame has faded, but senior citizens remember that he was a celebrated syndicated columnist in the 1930s. Look for a grave marker that looks like a granite park bench. To avoid getting lost, keep bearing left and you'll eventually find your way out of the cemetery.

Back on State 141, continue west about two miles and note Cemetery Church at the intersection of Township 342. It was once headquarters for the Methodist circuit-riding preacher. If you want to see the peaceful old cemetery here, turn right on Centenary Road.

Returning to State 141 for a half mile, watch for a left turn on Lincoln Pike, County 20. You'll see a Victorian house on the right and another picturesque home high on a hill to the left. The road follows Raccoon Creek for a spell. Its shimmering emerald green color comes from waters that run through the coal mines.

Cleanups are underway, and it's hoped that these creeks will once again yield a harvest of fish. Raccoon Creek once ran waterwheels that drove 13 mills. The creek sang with industry except when the wheels became so clogged with huge fish that they had to be cut away with axes.

Along the road, you'll see a log cabin, rugged forests, cows, and cornfields. Continue on Lincoln Pike, also called County 22 and Northup Road, until it dead-ends at State 775. Jog right, then immediately left on Dan Jones Road, which is also County 41. You'll see more of Raccoon Creek later at Bob Evans Farm, but this quiet, 700-acre reservation is a good place to stroll in the shadow of Poplar Knob, looking for bluebirds, ruffed grouse, deer, fox, and raccoon.

Only 12 miles from Gallipolis, the park, named Raccoon Creek County Park, is packed on summer weekends. Join in a baseball game on its huge playing fields, or come during the week or off-season to walk deserted hiking trails.

In springtime, the park is carpeted with trillium. A half-mile trail follows a natural gorge, and there also is a two-mile fitness trail and a 1.25-mile trail through Deer Hollow. The park is open all year.

Returning to State 775, continue south for less than a mile, watching for a right turn onto Patriot Road, leading to the village of Patriot (pronounced PAT-tree-ut, not PATE-tree-ut). The Patriot area and State 141 is growing rapidly into Southeastern Ohio's Amish country. Along 141, stop at Amish homes that put out shingles advertising their baked goods and handcrafted items, and at Aunt Clara's Collection of Fine Amish Things. Drive carefully, with a sharp eye for slow-moving buggies and for children walking to the Amish schools in this area.

Note Hannan Trace Road, County 50, which takes off south just before the center of the village. An ancient trail that dates to Indian times and was probably an animal trail before humans arrived, it winds its way south and eventually reaches the river.

A community sprang up here because this was the junction of the Hannan Trace and the Marietta-Portsmouth stagecoach route. Before the Civil War, it was a busy and prosperous community with its own silversmith, furniture makers, hotels, tannery, and mill that pulverized sassafras and shipped it by the barrelful to medicine makers. Until the 1950s, a kiln here processed locally grown tobacco. Tobacco, by the way, is still grown in southern Ohio. Watch for it, and for the occasional tobacco barn.

The most direct route to Rio (pronounced RYE-oh) Grande, which is only seven miles north of Patriot, is to head north on Gage Road, also called County 42, jog right on State 141, then immediately turn left on State 325. It's rich in scenery, with serene fields of tobacco, grazing Charolais cattle, and tidy farms. Here, as in so much of this region, barbed-wire fences are mounded high with tangles of multiflora roses— the farmer's scourge but a delight to tourists.

In addition to the route described, here are two side trips we took and recommend.

Side Trip One

Because this is part of Ohio's famous Hanging Rock iron district, waves of Welsh immigrants poured into this area early in the 19th century. To visit two of the churches built by the Welsh is a treat at any time, but it is a must when a traditional Welsh evening of speaking and song is being held. Such festivals are held only once or twice a year, but they bring in Welshmen from throughout Ohio.

Leave Patriot on Gage Road, turn right on State 141, left on State 325, and almost immediately take a left on Nebo Road. In two miles, turn left on Wolf Run and you'll see Nebos Church, one of the two sites favored for Welsh reunions.

Now go back east, staying on Wolf Run Road, turn left on State 325, and after a mile turn left on Centerpoint Road, County 48. The road dead-ends at Tyn Rhos Road. Turn right and, in less than a mile, you'll see the other church, Tyn Rhos (pronounced tin rose). There's a replica of the original immigrants' humble log house and a cemetery filled with Welsh names.

Tyn Rhos Road continues north to Cherry Ridge, County 44, and a right turn takes you the three miles into Rio Grande. As long as you've come this far on a Welsh pilgrimage, however, you may as well take one more detour. Stay with Tyn Rhos Road, Township 446, past Cherry Ridge and turn left on

Buckeye Hills Road through Centerville, where you'll pick up State 279 for an eight-mile drive to Oak Hill, in Jackson County.

Here, in the old Welsh Congregational Church on East Main Street, a Welsh-American Heritage Museum was founded in 1971. Relics relay the story of six families who set out from Aberaeron, Wales, in 1818. They sailed the Atlantic, hired covered wagons to take them across the mountains to Pittsburgh, then loaded their possessions aboard rafts for the journey down the Ohio River. They ran out of provisions by the time they reached Gallipolis, and there they went ashore to seek new homes in Ohio. More waves of Welsh settlers continued arriving in the area until about 1849.

Call the museum before visiting, because it is a small one and is likely to be closed except during special events.

Side Trip Two

From Patriot, go north on Gage Road, County 42, to State 141, then right for 1.5 miles, watching for a left turn on Maple Grove Road, County 34. Your goal is a crossroads called Cora, where a quaintly picturesque old mill was built along Raccoon Creek in 1835. Its wheel was swept away in the 1937 flood, but the scene along the creek and the old iron bridge is a lovely one. On a quiet day, you feel suspended in another century.

Sometimes a shingle is hung out at the red house opposite the mill, offering dried flowers, antiques, and gifts for sale. If the sisters who live there are home, you'll get a friendly reception.

Continue north on Cora Mill Road, County 12, for two miles to State 325. At Cora nothing remains of the once-busy community but a tidy church and the ruins of a store, but full corncribs are a sign that life is still good on these rich farmlands. A right turn on State 325 puts you back on course for the two-mile trip into Rio Grande.

If you like, park the car and wander around the shady campus of the University of Rio Grande, home of the Appalachian Institute for the Arts and Humanities. Many special music, art, and theater events are held here throughout the year.

State 325 takes you north from Rio Grande through rolling farms and forests, again across rambling Raccoon Creek, and into Vinton. It's about five miles. Just past the intersection of State 160, note the Morgan's Raid Historic Bridge in a tree-shaded park. The 140-foot suspension footbridge is a replica of the one that was burned here during the Civil War when Morgan's Raiders raided the town. Picnic in the park or just stroll along the creek.

Returning to Rio Grande on State 325, turn east (left) on State 588 and stop at Bob Evans Farm, which is open and free (except for a per-car admission during the October Farm Festival) April through October. Plan to have lunch or dinner at the General Store Restaurant here.

Bob Evans is best known for his nationwide restaurant chain that serves hearty country fare, but the Evans name also means horseback riding, canoeing, exploring Daniel Boone's Cave along Raccoon Creek, and touring a replica log-cabin village called Adamsville.

All six Evans children were raised on the old homestead, built in 1820 and once a stagecoach stop and inn. It's now on the National Register of Historic Places. Children love the wildlife area, and old-timers will feel at home in the farm museum and the log-cabin village. The sprawling complex is well worth an entire day of sightseeing. For an adventurous overnight, take a guided trail ride; campfire dinner and breakfast are included. Reservations are essential, so call ahead.

Returning to U.S. 35, which is a four-lane, divided highway in this area, head east and watch for the State 850 exit, where you'll see Jewel Evans' Grist Mill, a three-story masterpiece of Amish carpentry. Massive white-oak beams were chiseled by hand and fastened with wooden pegs.

Corn, cattle, and tobacco are this area's leading products today, but Jewel brings in the best hard winter wheat and a variety of grains from all over the land to create a ten-grain mixture that makes unforgettable breads, pancakes, and muffins. Also used in the products sold here are locally grown soft winter wheat, yellow corn, white corn, high-lysine corn, buckwheat, and oats.

The rare French buhr millstones that do the grinding came over as ballast in some of the first ships to ply the Ohio River. Grains, fresh breads, gift baskets, cereals, preserves, and other goodies are sold in the mill's country store. Although the mill is open all year, hours vary with the seasons. Admission is free.

Continuing east on U.S. 35, you may want to cross the river into West Virginia, noting that it's where the Kanawha River enters the Ohio River. On the West Virginia side of the bridge at Point Pleasant, an 84-foot granite shaft marks the spot where, it is agreed by Congress and historians, the first encounter of the American Revolution occurred.

Buried here with the military heroes is Ann Sargent Bailey, a deadeye shot and fearless scout in the Indian Wars. Born in England, she had married a soldier who was killed at the bloody battle of Point Pleasant in 1774. Donning buckskin and mounting a black stallion, she took his place, ghosting through trackless forests in Indian territory.

When Fort Clendenin was about to surrender for lack of ammunition, she sped to Lewisburg for powder and lead, and brought it back, past Indian sentries. The Indian Wars behind her and two husbands buried, she settled quietly in Gallipolis to teach Sunday School, drink whiskey, and nurse war veterans who were down on their luck. Locals considered her eccentric, and perhaps mad. When she died in 1825, she was buried at Point Pleasant. Mansion House, a log cabin built here in 1796 as a public inn, displays relics from the battle.

You're now just north of Gallipolis, our starting point.

For More Information

Ohio Valley Visitors Center of Gallia County (Gallipolis): 800-765-6482

Gallia County: 614-446-6882

Gallia County Historical Society and Gallia County Genealogical Society (Gallipolis): 614-446-7200

Cliffside Golf Course (Gallipolis): 614-446-GOLF (open to the public; greens fees are charged)

Our House State Memorial (Gallipolis): 614-446-0586 or 800-765-6482

French Art Colony Regional Multi-Arts Center (Gallipolis): 614-446-3834

Ariel Theatre (Gallipolis): 614-446-ARTS

French City Mall Crafts and Antiques (Gallipolis): 614-446-9020

Le Marquis Bistro and Lounge (Gallipolis): 614-446-2345

The Candle Shop Company (Gallipolis): 614-446-1603

Raccoon Creek County Park (Patriot): 614-379-2711

Aunt Clara's Collection of Fine Amish Things (Gallipolis): 614-446-0205

Welsh-American Heritage Museum (Oak Hill): 614-682-7057 or
614-682-7172

University of Rio Grande and Rio Grande Community College
(Rio Grande): 614-245-5353 or 800-282-7201

Bob Evans Farm (Rio Grande): 614-245-5305 or 800-944-FARM

Jewel Evans' Grist Mill: 614-245-5654

Index

About the Authors

Janet Hawkins Groene's grandfather descended from early settlers in Columbiana and Carroll Counties. As a mechanical engineer with Republic Steel, her father worked in Cleveland, Canton, and Youngstown during her childhood, eventually settling in Middleburg Heights. She went to Berea High School, then Baldwin-Wallace College, working summers for the *Berea News*. Later, she wrote for the *Cleveland Plain Dealer*.

Gordon Groene's family emigrated into northern Ohio from western New York. His grandfathers were artisans, one a mason and the other a glassworker, in the Cleveland area. His father's working years were spent with the old Fisher grocery chain.

Born in Parma, Gordon grew up in Middleburg Heights and graduated from Berea High School. It was natural for a northern Ohio boy to pursue a career in aviation, and he spent most of his teen years in his Luscombe, exploring the skies *above* Ohio's country roads. Later, as a professional pilot, Gordon flew out of Willoughby, Sandusky, then Youngstown before his career path took him and his wife to Illinois.

Now a full-time travel writer and photographer team who travel worldwide, the Groenes have published hundreds of newspaper and magazine articles and numerous books, including *Living Aboard Your* RV and *Cooking Aboard Your* RV (Ragged Mountain Press); *Romantic Weekends: Central and North Florida* (Hunter), and *Florida Guide, Caribbean Guide,* and *U.S. Caribbean Guide* (Open Road Publishing).

Their other Country Roads Press books include *Natural Wonders of Ohio*, *52 Florida Weekends*, and *Natural Wonders of Georgia*. Janet Groene's *Secrets of Successful Freelance Writing in the New Millenium* is published by BookHome, and the Groenes' *Great Eastern* RV *Trips* is published by Ragged Mountain Press.